D0890017

NEVER SAY YOU CAN'T SURVIVE

NEVER SAY YOU CAN'T SURVIVE

CHARLIE JANE ANDERS

A TOM DOHERTY ASSOCIATES BOOK
NEW YORK

NEVER SAY YOU CAN'T SURVIVE

Copyright © 2021 by Charlie Jane Anders

A Tordotcom Book
Published by Tom Doherty Associates
120 Broadway
New York, NY 10271

www.tor.com

Tor® is a registered trademark of Macmillan Publishing Group, LLC.

The Library of Congress Cataloging-in-Publication Data is available
upon request.

ISBN 978-1-250-80001-5 (hardcover)
ISBN 978-1-250-80002-2 (ebook)

Our books may be purchased in bulk for promotional, educational, or
business use. Please contact your local bookseller or the Macmillan Corporate
and Premium Sales Department at 1-800-221-7945, extension 5442, or by
email at MacmillanSpecialMarkets@macmillan.com.

First Edition: August 2021

Printed in the United States of America

0 9 8 7 6 5 4 3 2 1

For Annalee

NEVER SAY YOU CAN'T SURVIVE

INTRODUCTION

2020 was the worst year of my life, the same as for many other people. My father died of COVID-19, and this was part of a death toll that felt seismic, as if the landscape itself was being churned by overwhelming loss. I was coping with a cluster of family crises and struggling to finish a late book manuscript while trying to keep a dozen other commitments. And the world around me was nine kinds of messed up.

One thing got me through that hell-year: dreaming up imaginary worlds and larger-than-life people who never lived.

I was halfway through writing a young adult space fantasy trilogy, full of aliens and villains and starship battles and lots of kissing and people talking about their feelings—the first book, *Victories Greater Than Death,* is out now. Whenever I got overwhelmed with doomscrolling, I could escape by hanging out with Tina, Rachael, and Elza, and imagining how they overcame villainy and survived heinous dangers by being there for each other. At night, I crawled into bed with a blank journal and scribbled a fantasy novel for grown-ups until I fell asleep with my head full of spells.

Throughout that heinous year, I was also writing the essays in this book, which explain how you can use creative writing to survive the worst things history can throw at you.

Early in 2020, I had pitched the idea for a book about how to write your way out of hard times, which could be published in real-time installments at *Tor.com.* I could already tell that 2020 was going to be a uniquely heart-crushing time, and I hoped these essays would help a little.

Honestly? I had no earthly clue just how awful 2020 would

turn out to be, and how much I would need a space to think about the ways fiction could help me shield myself from harm. With the essays in this book, I was reminding myself, as much as anyone else, that writing can be an act of self-preservation. That creativity gives us heart and purpose and clarity and the ability to keep going. You can heal yourself just by making up your own fables.

(These essays came out of a talk that I gave at the Willamette Writers Conference and elsewhere. And this book's title, *Never Say You Can't Survive*, is borrowed from the 1977 album of the same name by Curtis Mayfield, which is a piece of music that has brought me so much strength and inspiration over the years.)

Putting any kind of story together makes you a god in your own private universe and grants you control over a whole world inside your own mind, even when the outside world feels like a constant torrent of awfulness.

You can use stories to face up to your most debilitating fears, the way I did with "Don't Press Charges and I Won't Sue" (see sidebar). Or you can turn to escapism and distract yourself with swashbuckling tales of action and romance, the way I did with *Victories Greater Than Death*. You can also combine the two: wrapping escapist fun around a kernel of real-life politics.

People sometimes talk about escapist storytelling as a kind of dereliction of duty—as if we're running away from the fight. That's some garbage right there, because escapism *is* resistance. In her 1979 essay collection *The Language of the Night*, Ursula K. Le Guin paraphrases Tolkien: "If a soldier is captured by the enemy, don't we consider it his duty to escape? . . . If we value the freedom of the mind and soul, if we're partisans of liberty, then it's our plain duty to escape and to take as many people with us as we can."

Visualizing a happier, more just world is a direct assault on the forces that are trying to break your heart. As Le Guin says elsewhere, the most powerful thing you can do is imagine how things could be different . . . What if?

It's no accident that some of the most enduring and positive communities in the real world have come out of people sharing an escapist narrative. *Star Trek, Doctor Who, Star Wars, Steven Universe, She-Ra,* and countless other series have created wonderful real-life fellowships. Happier, kinder worlds in fiction naturally lead people to band together, to try and create pockets of that experience in our world. And there's plenty of evidence that these fan communities feed directly into political organizing.

But that's about how escapism can be helpful for readers. Let's get back to how it can be good for you, the writer.

People will always try to control you by constraining your sense of what's possible. They want to tell you that reality consists of only the things that they are willing to recognize, and anything else is foolishness.

But you can reject their false limitations in the act of conjuring your own world—and carve out a pocket of your mind that *they* cannot touch, in the act of world-building. The more details you add to your world, the realer it feels in your mind. And thus, the better refuge it can become during hard times.

I know a lot of people who haven't been able to keep writing these past few years. It's hard to know what the point is of making up random stories when everything is messed up. Families are still being destroyed every day by institutionalized racism, there's an endless debate over whether trans people deserve to have any rights at all, and women's healthcare is slipping backward. Many of us feel like our very personhood is up for grabs. During the bleakest moments of 2020, I found it impossible to motivate myself, and there were days when I didn't write a single word.

And yet, the more I thought of storytelling as a safe place

to work through my feelings, and a sanctuary for my mind, the easier it was to put the real world away and turn to the (way cooler) world inside my head.

How getting better at writing can help you survive the worst

You never stop learning how to do better at writing—even if you've published a bunch of books and "arrived" as an author, you're still on a steep learning curve, for as long as you're stringing words together. This is excellent, because it means there will always be new discoveries and insights. Put another way, if writing was a house, you would never run out of rooms to explore.

The essays in this book are a mixture of encouragement, ideas for how to use writing to feel okay in a world that is not okay, and actual technical advice on stuff like characters, plotting, and world-building.

In the first section, "Getting Started," I talk right away about creating characters—because your protagonist(s) can provide you with a whole alternate consciousness. When you create a fictional person, you're making a whole other

TURN YOUR FEARS INTO STORIES

Back in January 2017, I was scared out of my wits. I was having trouble sleeping and suffering panic attacks about the impending inauguration of Donald Trump, and the ways he would try to deny safety and equality to trans people. I couldn't concentrate on finishing *The City in the Middle of the Night,* until I finally decided to channel all of my anxiety into a story about my fears as a trans woman.

The result, "Don't Press Charges and I Won't Sue," is a dystopian nightmare about a trans woman who gets captured by an evil NGO and forced to undergo a surreal, exaggerated "cure" for her transness. It's horrifying and intense—and I've only read it aloud once, because I find the words too painful to speak. A number of other trans people have told me that they needed to lie down after reading it.

But putting my fears into a story really helped me to deal with them, and I've heard from some cis people that this story helped them understand what trans people are facing.

When I wrote "Don't Press Charges and I Won't Sue," I was going to the darkest possible place, and putting my protagonist through the most dehumanizing treatment I could imagine. I needed to face up to the absolute worst that could happen, so I felt like I understood it a little better. I also needed to imagine someone surviving the most nightmarish scenario and breaking free, even though it's a dark ending.

This wasn't the first time I used fiction to cope with political anxieties—after the 2004 election, I guest-edited a special issue of a queer erotica journal, full of stories about LGBTQIA+ people joining together to process their feelings about a second term for George W. Bush. And I wrote a handful of dystopian stories in the mid-2000s, about my fears that hyper-capitalism and income inequality could end up harming trans and queer people in ways that most bigots could only dream of.

Writing a horrifying story on

persona, or even an alternate self. Instead of living your own life, you can be immersed in someone else's.

And the rest of the early essays are about giving yourself permission to write—and that, in turn, means rejecting imposter syndrome and accepting that you're going to make mistakes. Mistakes are awesome, especially if they lead you in a surprising direction.

For me, a good writing day is often one where something happens in my story that I never saw coming and didn't plan on. When my characters take on a life of their own, or when I find pockets of my world that I never knew were there, it's magical. Even as I'm learning new things about how to tell a story, I love to feel like I'm also learning more about my characters and world as I go. (And speaking of which, research can also be an underrated fun part of writing, because you learn the weirdest facts—that you can then inflict on all your loved ones.)

Then there's the second section, "What's a Story and How Do You Find One?" Identifying the story that you want to tell can be ridiculously fun, when it's not making you want to tear your hair out. The moment when you get excited about a premise, and then start building out the world and the characters, is bloody magic.

The third section is all about harnessing the awesome power of your own emotions—and not letting anyone tell you that your feelings aren't valid. Or that you're dealing with them the wrong way.

If you're depressed, don't try to force yourself out of it—and don't try to make yourself write something that you're not feeling up to.

your own terms means that you can show how someone can endure, or even triumph. And meanwhile, you can cast a light on the injustice of oppressive systems. You get to choose the frame and eliminate some of the ambiguity, to make things starker and more clear, or to make juxtapositions that illuminate how the problem started, and how it'll be in the future.

When you're telling the story, you get to draw all the lines.

Whether you feel like writing light and fluffy escapist stories, or dark and intense tales of suffering and angst, it's all good. Whatever you are able to write in this tough time is self-evidently the right project for you.

If you're angry, stay angry. Anger is the best fuel for writing, emotion, plot, comedy, and everything else. Channel that energy into stories. Use your anger to create something so beautiful, people will cry all over the page.

And if you feel like writing erotica, write erotica. Make it dirty and obnoxious and queer and sweet and righteous, and build a fortress of horniness to protect you from this cold, ugly world.

Dive into endless world-building, and create more and more elaborate systems and histories, if that makes you feel excited.

For me, I get the most joy from writing about relationships. The tiniest moments of personal connection can feel huge as you're writing them. I try to remember to luxuriate in the little moments, like when two characters haven't seen each other in ages and they're together again, and I have a chance to write a quiet emotional scene between them.

And the fourth section, "What We Write About When We Write About Spaceships," delves more into how to use your fiction to process the trauma of living through a moment when the whole world turns into flaming walls of shit.

Don't be afraid to be political in your writing, but don't feel any obligation to champion any particular ideal or point of view. Politics is bound to show up, one way or another, and it's important to be mindful about the politics of your story—but you don't have to be political in the way that anyone else expects.

You don't have to think of yourself as an activist—but anyone who imagines a different reality is helping everyone else to see our power to act, and to make changes. Imagination is always a form of resistance to domination and oppression, and we've all been saved by other people's stories one time or another. There's a reason why politicians and organizers try to tell stories, to put a human face on their policies, and worry about "controlling the narrative"—it's because our world is built out of stories.

And then there's the power of telling stories about people who haven't gotten to be the heroes of our stories in the past. If you're a member of a marginalized or oppressed group, putting someone like yourself into a story can be incredibly powerful, as I found when I started writing stories about trans and queer characters. In one chapter, I talk about the importance of representation without appropriation—or how we can reflect the diversity of the real world in our stories without telling stories that aren't ours to tell. The past few years have shown us how powerful representation is, in the midst of a tidal wave of hatred and bigotry.

The issue of representation in fiction is not just some academic question of fairness, it's a matter of survival. When the full diversity of people is represented in stories, it expands people's sense of possibility. It's incredible how direct a line there is from representation in fiction to empowerment in the real world. And celebrating cultures that have been historically suppressed or downgraded is a powerful act.

The final section is called "How to Use Writerly Tricks to Gain Unstoppable Powers," and it's the most nuts-and-bolts part of the book.

A lot of fancy writing techniques are basically ways for you to gain more control over this imaginary realm you've created with your mind. You get to choose who's telling the story, how close we are to your characters' points of view, whether the story is past tense or present tense, and what details the reader pays attention to.

Playing with the passage of time, speeding it up and slowing it down, can be a way to show the arc of history and demonstrate that things that appear permanent really aren't. Or to reveal the wealth of experience and sustenance that can exist within a single profound moment. All of these things make you more powerful as a storyteller, and in turn make the act of storytelling more restorative.

Because you can shape every aspect of a story, you can use perspective and irony to expose the true awfulness of a situation—or to provide hope for another way. You can pull back and show the big picture, the long view, through narrative choices that reveal all the stuff that the main character isn't seeing. You can provide context through expansive narration.

And irony is amazingly powerful, because it works against groupthink and paranoia. Fear is about tunnel vision—and you don't have to limit your perspective that way when you're the one controlling the focus.

That voice inside you that stands back and analyzes everything from a distance? It's so often key to surviving in the midst of scary and depressing moments. You can give that voice its own place at the center of the narrative. I love a chatty, sarcastic first-person narrator—or, for that matter, a chatty, sarcastic third-person narrator.

There's a reason so much of the most powerful writing from survivors of horrifying events contains surreal or unreal elements. People who have been through unthinkable ordeals often instinctively take refuge in weird, reality-warping scenarios, and you can totally make this work for you. Normality is *bullshit,* and surrealist weirdness is a direct assault on the bullshit fortress.

We're all made of stories

Writing is a solitary act—but it's also a way to feel connected to the world, in a different way than spending ten hours a day on social media. When you write, you always have an imaginary reader in your head, but you also get to be part of a community of writers, each reading each other's work and building on each other's ideas, and supporting each other through all the frustrations and setbacks.

And your stories, too, can be full of communities coming together and supporting each other (and occasionally being obnoxious as hell). Lately, whenever I talk about worldbuilding, I always focus on how a good fictional world has strong communities—and I'm honestly tired of stories where there's the protagonist and then there's just a painted backdrop behind them, that's only there for them to react against. We are shaped by our communities, for good and bad, and our communities define the worlds we belong to.

Community is going to save us in real life—and in fiction, stories about communities joining together are going to be a lifeline.

You might set out to write a story just to save yourself, which is a noble and worthwhile goal—but in the process, you might just end up helping to save other people, too. Your characters' struggles can remind other people that no struggle is ever futile, and your "found family" of supporting characters can help readers to feel less alone. You can tell stories that span days or centuries, that travel vast distances or explore the secrets of a single location—and, most of all, that contain startling discoveries and acts of generosity.

You have the power to shape worlds, and the monsters are scared of you.

SECTION I

GETTING
STARTED

CHAPTER 1

How to Make Your Own Imaginary Friends

A huge part of the pleasure of creating stories is having another consciousness inside your own head. As soon as you invent a fictional character (or even a story that represents a real person), you're getting lost in that other perspective.

There's something both weird and tyrannical about being a person and getting stuck in just one point of view all the time. Everyone has that experience sometimes where you wake up from a vivid dream and for a moment you don't remember where you are and what's been going on. Everything from your skin outward feels like a blank slate, with infinite possibilities, until reality comes smashing back down onto you.

But when you have other people living inside your head, it's a way to have that same feeling when you're fully awake.

I think of it as being like when you have a hard drive, and you partition it—so instead of one drive, you have two, occupying the same piece of hardware. That's kind of what it can be like when you create a character and they come to life. They take over their own separate space inside your head. Sometimes it's just a relief to be someone else for a while.

One time, when I was recovering from surgery, I binged an entire season of *The Flash* to distract myself, and I found great consolation in obsessing about Cisco and Iris and Wally instead of my own nasty bandages. I've definitely gotten lost in reading other people's books, too. But getting immersed in my own writing project is the best way I've found to get out of my own reality.

Think of it as "hanging out with your imaginary friends."

Get curious

So how do you find your way into that headspace of living vicariously through the fake people you've created?

To me, it often starts with becoming curious. I try to find a person, a place, or a set of events that I want to know more about—and the only way to find out more is to keep pulling on the threads and coming up with the answers myself, out of my own imagination. This is a process that reinforces itself, because the harder you pull at the loose threads, the more threads there are to pull at.

The thing that makes you want to keep writing is the exact same thing that makes you want to keep reading—you want to see where this goes. You want to spend more time with these people and you want to understand what's really going on behind the curtain. Even if you've planned out your story meticulously, you need to see how these events actually play out. (And as I mentioned previously, part of the joy of writing is being surprised.)

Often, when I'm creating a character, I try to find that loose thread. It could be a contradiction at the heart of their personality, which I want to resolve or understand. It could be one random detail about the character that I fixate on. Often, it's the situation that the character finds themself in, or the conflict that they're trying to resolve. And finding a way to root for this character (they're the underdog! they want to right some wrong! they're treated unfairly!) goes hand in hand with becoming curious about them.

As with all writing advice, your mileage may vary—but for me, it's not about knowing every little thing about a character at the start. I don't need to know their favorite brand of toothpaste, or what kind of socks they wear. I often layer in those little details as I write, or more likely as I revise. When I'm starting out, boring details make me bored, but I cling fervently to the aspects of a character that "pop" and bring up more questions. Like, if a character carries around a watch chain with no watch, or spits every time you mention Winston Churchill, or can't resist getting drawn into magical duels, I want to know more.

Embrace change

In the meantime, I get more curious and engaged with a character who isn't static. The sooner I can see a character going through changes, the better—because often, your characters are only as compelling as the changes they go through. There's a reason why so many novels begin on the day when their protagonist's life is altered forever, rather than starting out with everything on an even keel. When you've seen a character evolve once, you know they can do it again. And again.

I'm a big believer in superhero-style origin stories, even if they never appear in the final manuscript. Not so much in terms of "how did they get their powers?" as "what happened to motivate them?" What was the thing that made this character decide to do what they're doing? What challenges have they faced before?

When I was writing *All the Birds in the Sky,* I came up with origin stories for every single character in the story—even minor ones, like Kanot or Dorothea—and tried to see how they were different people in the past than they are now. (And I was inspired by the flashbacks in the TV show *Lost,* which always showed drastically different versions of the characters than their present-day selves.)

Here's a quick writing exercise: Write down just one paragraph about something intense that happened to you in the past. Pretend you're telling a friend about a situation that tested you, and upset you, and maybe also brought out some valor in you. And then think about the fact that you're no longer the person who went through that mess—you're almost writing about a different person. And by retelling that story, you're both reliving and recontextualizing those events. And maybe try to fictionalize some of the details and see how it becomes more and more about a different person.

The next thing you know, you're turning yourself into a story. And you're also spending a moment with the two different parts of yourself that come into play when you're tormenting your characters.

There's the you that's standing outside the story and thinking of ways to make life miserable for these people, and then there's the you that's inhabiting them and going through their desperate struggle with them. These two parts of yourself aren't really at odds, they're both weaving a story together—and this actually makes you feel bigger, because you can contain them both. Bigger, and more alive, in a world that wants you to be small and half-dead.

And speaking of change and origin stories, there's something incredibly compelling about a character who has major regrets. And when we watch someone do something unforgivable, we're primed to root for them as they search desperately for an impossible forgiveness. I also live for a character who has unfinished business, something from their past that nags at them.

A good character usually has as much story behind them as ahead of them. We might only need to glimpse their past, but we should know that they've already been on the journey before the story even begins.

Think about what your character isn't seeing

I love self-aware characters, and characters who comprehend a situation in ways that nobody else does. There's something very satisfying about identifying with the only person who's aware of a problem that everyone else ignores.

And yet, often the easiest characters to invest in are the ones who are blissfully (or excruciatingly) unaware of what's going on around them. People who are in denial, or selectively oblivious. People who have been kept in the dark about some basic facts of their own lives. Especially when we can glimpse things out of the corner of our eyes that these characters fail to notice, it can create a kind of suspense—like in a horror movie, when you want to shout *look behind you*!—and fill you with a desperate urge to see this person wake up to reality.

When I was writing *The City in the Middle of the Night,* one of the ways that I got into Mouth's POV was by putting her self-image at odds with her reality. Right off the bat, you learn that she thinks of herself as someone who loves constant travel—but the road gives her headaches and makes her miserable. She describes herself as a remorseless killer—but she agonizes nonstop about whether she should have killed Justin, the fence who betrayed her. She's not the person she keeps telling herself she is, and that made me want to know more about her.

On a similar note, I've got all the time in the world for someone who's having an identity crisis.

Pretty much every protagonist I've ever created has been struggling with the question of "Who am I?" Or, to put it another way, "What does this make me?" When a character is struggling with a huge choice, they're really trying to figure out who they'll become if they do this, versus that. How can they use whatever power they have wisely? How can they rise above the terrible circumstances that threaten to break them?

Meanwhile, to turn it around, I often find that when a character isn't clicking, it's because I'm avoiding the biggest pain points, because nobody likes to dwell on unpleasant things.

Why isn't this character upset by the death of their mother? Why did this character never have a real reaction to their friend's betrayal? Why isn't anyone calling this person on their bad behavior? I sometimes instinctively flinch away from the most intense parts of a character's story—and I've seen this in plenty of books I've read, too. When I realize my mind is sliding away from some aspect of a character, that's usually where the really good stuff is. (And I talk a bit more about this later on, in the chapter on turning fake emotion into real emotion.)

Some more ideas for finding the perfect imaginary friend

Give your character a strong point of view. Make them funny, give them ironic observations about their situation, let them vent a healthy dose of snark. You're going to want to spend time with whoever has the funniest lines and darkest insights, whether that person is the first-person narrator, third-person POV, or just someone we hear from. Master storyteller Eileen Gunn says that when a character isn't clicking, she usually gets them to rant about something. Basically, do whatever you have to do to get this character's voice in your head: write a fiery monologue, talk to yourself in the shower, have them livetweet their favorite TV show. Whatever. Doesn't hurt if your character is a little bit of an obnoxious asshole. Or a lot of one.

Put your character at odds with their world. Similarly, there's something immediately compelling about a character who disagrees with everyone else. In a world where everyone wears psychic snakes as belts, it's more interesting to follow the one person who loathes snakes. Maybe your character is part of a whole community of outcasts, or maybe they're a lone rebel—but it's always easier to invest in someone who doesn't entirely fit in, and who might see the injustices everyone else chooses to ignore.

Start with a type and then mess them up. Often, a good character starts off as an archetype that you've seen before in fiction (or in real life). But the more time you spend with them and the more different situations you put them in, the more they start to open up and show different layers that you might not have expected from the broad-brush characterization you originally gave them. This is really no different from how you get to know living, breathing people. You start with a label— "gamer," "yuppie," "crust punk"—and then gradually you find out that there's more to this person than their category. The good thing about meeting characters as types first is that you can start them off loud and exaggerated—like a dashing rogue, or a cowardly spy—and let them make a strong impression. And then you can find the subtlety inside them later. (Sometimes they get deeper and more layered in revision, too. But we'll talk about revision later.)

Start with an intense situation and then figure out who's in it. Someone stole your shoes. Your mother got trapped in a collapsed railway tunnel. You finally got a shot at your dream job, but the interview was a disaster. You got thrown out of an airplane without a parachute. If the situation is intense enough, you can be swept along by it, and then you can find your character by how they react to this mess they're in.

Give your protagonist a goal they can never have. Make your characters sweat, right off the bat. We can all think of compelling fictional characters who don't seem to want anything much—but as a general rule, we care about people who have strong goals. And there's nothing better than a character who wants something that's actually impossible, like staying young forever or winning the love of someone who's totally unavailable. (Or see above, re: impossible forgiveness.)

Imagine an extreme action and then try to picture the person doing it. This sort of goes hand in hand with characters being at odds with their society, and also the thing about launching the story on the day that everything changes. Sometimes the best way to get into a character is to see them do something completely outrageous, something that nobody else would choose to do—and then find out why, and what the consequences are. What do you *mean,* you fed your psychic snakebelt to the great mongoose who lives in the forbidden zone? What kind of maniac *are you*?

We all contain multitudes

When I was in college, I took a year off and lived in China and Australia. I supported myself by teaching English in Beijing, and by working in warehouses in Sydney, and I found out that I was a very different person when I was standing in front of a classroom than when I was hauling boxes around. (And don't get me started on that time that I nearly got stabbed by my tweaker roommate, who then sicced a biker gang on me. Long story.)

The point is, I got a really good sense of how different I could be, depending on where I was and what I was doing. And since then, I've had a few different careers and transitioned from male to female. At the same time, there's a part of me that never changes: my core or whatever.

We all contain many wildly divergent versions of ourselves, which is part of why creating characters and making up stories is so exciting and fulfilling. It's a way to discover new aspects of your own mind and create personas that you get to inhabit for a period of time. And these figments of your imagination won't just keep you company in the midst of an atrocity, they'll also help you to strengthen your mind. You can gain courage from these made-up struggles against adversity and also find out that there's more to you than anyone ever realized.

When your characters take on a life of their own, they can help give you life. And maybe, in turn, you can put them out into the world, so they can give some life to everyone else. We all need an imaginary posse every now and then.

CHAPTER 2

Imposter Syndrome Is Just
Part of Being a Writer

You can never know what your stories are worth.

When you put a story out in the world, you won't ever know who's read it, or how many readers there were, or what it's meant to them. A single copy of a book can get passed around and shared and picked up, over and over again.

Nobody is ever going to come along with a magic wand and say, "You're a real writer now." There are a million definitions of writing success out there, and almost everyone feels like a failure sometimes. (Constantly, in my case.)

You're not competing with other writers. The first thing people do when they finish reading a book they enjoyed is search for more books like that one. Your biggest competition is always the dreaded "reading slump," when people just fall out of the habit of reading because they haven't found the right book for them lately. Anything, or anyone, who gets people reading is good for all of us.

Nevertheless, imposter syndrome is everywhere, and so are gatekeepers who want to tell you that you're doing it wrong. Everyone has their own supposedly ironclad rules for writing—and if you let this stuff get you down, you'll find it harder to write. You definitely won't be able to use writing to find liberation, or to see a better future, if you're worrying about whether you're "allowed" to do this, or whether your work matters.

You can banish imposter syndrome, and the insecurity that lies behind it, by finding the communities of people who want to give each other props and encourage each other to concoct better dreams. Take pleasure in whatever aspects of writing (and publishing) you can enjoy right now, even if that's just knowing that you crafted one really kick-ass sentence today. And most of all, don't listen to insecure people who try to impose conditions on being a "real writer."

The moment you wrote down a single word, you became a real writer. Really.

Imposter syndrome is forever

The bad news is, imposter syndrome never really goes away. But that's also the good news. Aside from a handful of exceptions, everybody who's writing and publishing and doing appearances is plagued by imposter syndrome.

Imposter syndrome can be a sign that you're doing well, because you always feel more insecure when you're starting to get more recognition. It's also a chance to stretch your imagination—because you're sort of playing make-believe until you actually believe you're a writer—and a way to build empathy for other struggling writers. Being honest about imposter syndrome is also a great way to connect with other people in the same boat.

At its root, imposter syndrome is a fear of not living up to the role of "author"—a one-size-fits-all garment that doesn't suit anybody perfectly. It's bound to pinch in some areas, and poof out in others. The same is probably true with any other professional identity: if you were a seismologist, you'd have people judging you on whether you wear the right kind of quake-proof shoes, and how well you know your subduction zones by heart. (I'm guessing.)

The main difference is, we've built up a lot of mystique about writers, including a lot of romantic notions and glamorous archetypes that have little to do with reality. A lot of writers are overly invested in keeping the mystery alive—like, people are shy about admitting the financial and other support they received that allowed them to do this. (Full disclosure: my parents supported me through college and gave me some help when I was starting out—so while I did have a full-time day job until recently, I did not have to pay off a mountain of student loans.)

Speaking of money . . . if you don't get paid (or paid enough) for your writing, you might also get force-fed the idea that you're not a real author. In fact, two seemingly opposite things are true:

· Writers should get paid for their work.
· Writers who don't get paid are still real writers.

During my painful first decade of trying to be a writer, I mostly published my work in small-press publications, which paid a small amount (or, in some cases, paid in copies). And for a while there, I was posting my stories on message boards, or taking part in group story-writing projects, where nobody got paid. Truth is, even if you achieve more financial success, a lot of the work that writers do is emotional labor, which never gets compensated.

We all know that some of the most valuable work you can do is unpaid, and a lot of the work that you get paid for is worthless. I found that out firsthand when I temped in my early twenties, and was literally paid to "look busy" for days at a time, including one job where I was reprimanded for getting my work done too quickly. Another time, I was paid to be a "receptionist" with a disconnected phone and a dead computer, because these hedge-fund managers wanted a receptionist as a status symbol—but they also wanted to answer their own phones.

So getting paid is essential—but it's not what makes you a real writer.

When you peel back the layers of insecurity behind imposter syndrome, you find a lot of preconceptions about what an author should act like, sound like, or look like, which come out of the class, race, gender, and other stratifications in our society. I've literally had people tell me you can't be a real author unless you have the right kind of expensive haircut. (And nah, my pink bob isn't what they had in mind.)

There are plenty of social situations where you might feel like a fraud, but imposter syndrome is especially a problem if it keeps you from being able to write. Or keeps you from tackling the projects you really want to create, because you doubt your own capabilities. We'll talk about what to do when you hate your own writing in another chapter—but for now, just know that if there's one thing that absolutely makes you a "real writer," it's having a bad writing day.

Screw the rules

Seriously. People will try to tell you "the rules" of writing, and it's all nonsense. (And if you ever catch me saying anything that looks like a "rule" in these chapters, you are cordially encouraged to smack me upside the head.)

You mustn't write second-person narrators. You can't include prologues, or maybe prologues are mandatory. No omniscient POV. You must write every single day—preferably at both dawn and dusk, while perched on top of the carcass of a freshly butchered Norwegian snow lynx. No adverbs! Every time you introduce a new character, you must give them a comical nickname, like "Batwing-Pants McDougal." Only mention eyebrows when they are raised, or you will ruin foreheads for everyone.

And so on.

I get why people want to share their own writing rules—as I mentioned, we're all super insecure, and you never really know if anyone's going to like a particular piece of writing. None of us have that much control over the things we care most about, so we cling to the illusion that we know some universal laws of authordom. Plus, when you find something that works for you, it's natural to want to share it with everyone else, and to overcompensate by presenting it as more than just a suggestion.

Nevertheless, rulemaking is another way that we internalize our anxieties, and then put them on everyone else. Nobody ever wants to admit how confused we all are. To make matters worse, there's a lot of intentional mystification around writing, to make a messy, clunky, trial-and-error process feel more like some kind of secret ritual that ensures success. When really, we're all just stumbling around, walking into walls over and over.

Status nonsense

Imposter syndrome doesn't come out of nowhere—it comes from real experiences of people trying to tell us that we don't belong. I asked people on Twitter about their worst experiences of authorial imposter syndrome—and I was startled by the sheer number of stories people shared about microaggressions and overt gatekeeping.

Unfortunately, speculative fiction is full of people trying to remind you of your place in some imaginary pecking order. Many years ago, I was overjoyed to get one of my stories into a small-press anthology, which also featured a few "big name" authors. At the launch party, I read my story, and one well-known author read his. Afterward, that author, whom I'd met a few times before, came up to me and said, "Your story was much better than I expected it to be." Then he paused and, as if wanting to make sure his message had gotten through, he leaned forward and said, "No, really. I didn't expect it to be that good."

Everyone has had experiences like that. You can blame some of this behavior on social awkwardness, for sure, but a lot of it is also due to an overinvestment in some idea of a star system, when really we're all in one slightly leaky boat together.

The world is full of famous authors that you've never heard of. I've been running my own reading series in a bar for nearly two decades, and I've found that someone who's a "big name" in one genre or scene is a total unknown to readers and writers in an adjacent scene. I've also discovered that authors who have a strong community behind them are better off, in the long run, than ones who achieve some "mainstream" success.

We need to stop putting a handful of authors on pedestals, because it's not healthy for anybody. Where there's one author doing a cool new spin on postmodern ghost stories, there's always a whole group of people doing that same thing and getting less attention.

This is all so much harder for science fiction and fantasy writers, because the outside world still views SF as an inferior, cheesetastic genre. That's changing, but not quite fast enough. Then we turn around and impose genre snobbery on each other—like, some science fiction is "harder" than others, often for reasons unrelated to the science content of the story. Or science fiction is better than fantasy, for reasons. We find reasons to look down on science fiction romance, or space opera, while chasing the latest trendy subgenre.

This is especially shitty when it leads to self-censorship—or worse, people getting creatively blocked because they don't feel like they're allowed to write the book they want to write.

Again, you never really know what a story is worth, or who will discover it and fall in love with it. Every writer is just throwing stuff out there and seeing what sticks to the wall, and we all have hits and misses. Everyone remembers Frank Herbert's *Dune,* but nobody is reading *Destination: Void.*

Find the people who support you

I came up with a life hack years ago, for when I find myself talking to someone who wants to obsess about status, and who's up and who's down.

At the soonest polite moment, I break in and ask, "Hey, what book have you been enjoying lately?" This never fails: the conversation turns to this incredible book that this person discovered, and how cool it is, and how it reminds them of five other awesome books. We all love to geek out about books, even more than we love to find ways to treat this endless struggle to create and publish like some kind of March Madness bracket. (And as an aside, I really do think some of this obsession with status comes out of the fact that it's fun to nerd out about stats and points, because we also love gaming.)

Even people who sometimes behave obnoxiously share that same love of speculative fiction, and that awareness that we're a community of booklovers—or really, a set of countless intersecting communities.

None of us can do our best work unless we're all supporting and encouraging each other, so you need to find the people who appreciate you and want to pull you up with them when they're doing well. During that aforementioned decade of struggling in obscurity, I found out the hard way that having friends and colleagues and chosen family around was essential to my sanity as a writer. But also, those people made writing more fun and helped me to dream bigger and weirder.

Here's the definition of "success" I came up with years ago, which I try to hold fast to. I consider myself successful if:

- I get to work with people I like and admire, on projects that I am excited about.
- I get to keep writing and having people read my stuff.

I strongly encourage you to find a definition of success that makes you happy, rather than encouraging you to be miserable. And then stick to it, no matter what.

As I go on, the first half of that definition gets more important, not less. When I want to know if I'm doing well, I look at the people around me and see that they're badass weirdos whose work keeps surprising and thrilling me. It sounds sappy, but we're there for each other. Whatever you're writing and however you do it, there are other people out there who will share your ideas, and your ideals. They will be a lifeline when imposter syndrome starts to get in the way of your creative flow.

I spent several months in LA, where there are actual famous people all over the place and it's easy to get reminded that we're all just book people. There was a big tequila ad, towering over Hollywood, that said "FAME IS FLEETING." For a month or so the first "E" was burned out, so it read "FAM IS FLEETING".

I remember looking up at it and saying, "Nah. Fam is forever."

CHAPTER 3

The Teacher Who Saved My Life
(and Made Me a Writer)

The very first time that creative writing helped me to survive, I was just six years old.

I had a severe learning disability in elementary school—I nearly flunked out of first grade, second grade, and third grade. I couldn't hold a pencil right, no matter how many times people showed me, and when I tried to put words on paper, the outcome was an unreadable jumble. I sat and stared at my blank notebook page, inhaling the scent of stale PB&J crumbs and spilt chocolate milk, while the teacher got more frustrated and the other kids made fun of me.

Then a brand-new special education teacher took me under her wing. Lynn Pennington saved my life, and started me on the path that led to becoming a writer.

Ms. Pennington spent hours and hours with me, trying to help me get around the mental block that made me struggle with not just penmanship, but being able to form words at all. I remember feeling as if a blight slowly lifted.

I'm still friends with Ms. Pennington today—I will always call her Ms. Pennington—and she recently sent me some photos of me as a first-grader, gazing dolefully at a blank page. She's filled in some of the gaps in my memory, and I've realized there was more to the story than I knew at the time.

Like, I never knew just how frustrated my teachers were, and how much they complained about me in the teachers' lounge. I could read ahead of my grade level, but Ms. Pennington spent ages teaching me to hold a pencil the right way, and to recognize the difference between proper letters and the squiggles I was creating. A lot of people would have just run drills—making me write a hundred letter A's, until I got it right—but Ms. Pennington coaxed me to do one decent A, and then helped me recognize why it was correct. She was working on "perceptual formation," as she puts it now.

I was this heedless daydreamer, a mumbling oddity who slouched around the schoolyard making up stories in my head instead of talking to other kids. I had imaginary friends, and imaginary adventures, and a whole imaginary life. Ms. Pennington turned my tendency to daydream into a tool for getting me to learn. And in the process, she made me into a lifelong storytelling addict.

Ms. Pennington gave me lots of gold stars and praise, when I got a letter right, but she also offered me a much bigger bribe. If I mastered all my writing skills and got up to speed on my classwork, then I could write a play—and we'd get it performed at school. Eventually, toward the end of first grade, I wrote a play called *The Bad Cad,* and to hear Ms. Pennington tell it now, she could see my writing become smoother and more legible the more I worked on it.

The story of this play was basically what it sounds like: the Bad Cad is a troublemaker, who goes around wreaking havoc and screwing with an uptight authority figure (who was my older brother). She recently sent me some photos of the one and only performance of *The Bad Cad,* and you can see my face lighting up on stage. This was probably my first ever work of creative writing.

My mom recently told me that she was in a group of parents back then, and she heard one of the moms brag to the others that her child was in Ms. Pennington's special needs class. Because, my mom says, the word had gotten around that there was this one teacher giving all one-on-one attention to the learning-disabled kids. And this had become a status symbol among the trendy parents at Southeast Elementary School.

Ms. Pennington made me feel safe at school, and less like a Problem Child. I would sit in her lap and hug her, and I drew her pictures of Bert and Ernie from *Sesame Street,* with messages like "I like having you as a teacher." She was the first authority figure who didn't try to punish me for the difficulties I was having. Because even after *The Bad Cad,* I kept making all my other teachers see red.

In second grade, Ms. Pennington came up with another project for me. I would create a fake newspaper, which mostly consisted of silly political cartoons—I may or may not still have a photocopy someplace of my fake broadsheet, with a ridiculous political cartoon showing the President's "Cabinet" (full of outlandish kitchenwares).

As a reward, she took me out of school for a day, and we went to Hartford, a forty-five-minute drive away, and we toured the headquarters of the *Hartford Courant,* just the two of us. I remember seeing the sprawling offices, but also the big printing press, with the comically huge rolls of paper. (In the late 90s, I went to work for a newspaper and found that it had an identical printing press, with identical paper rolls, in its basement.)

I never got particularly good at elementary school. Once I could actually write semi-legibly, I spent my time scribbling *Doctor Who* fanfic in all of my school workbooks—this is one of the things I remember from back then, and apparently it made an impression on other people. "You were off in your *Doctor Who* world, when you should have been doing some work," was one of the first things Ms. Pennington told me, when I called her up to ask her some questions about that time in our lives.

I never for a second believed, as a child, that my disability made me any less the hero in my own story, and I give all the credit to Ms. Pennington for that. This was a formative experience for me, and I can't even imagine what sort of person I would be today if I hadn't come away from that time in my life with the lesson that the answer to severe impediments was to come up with the silliest ideas I could, and ride them all the way home.

CHAPTER 4

Embrace Uncertainty: the Joy
of Making a Giant Mess

I can still remember the last time I felt like a total confused noob as a writer.

It was a couple weeks ago.

I had just begun writing a brand-new story, and realized that I still know nothing about how to start things. That blank white screen was taunting me with its milky emptiness, and I couldn't find a way in. I had some neat ideas, a vague sense of an opening scene, a sliver of a main character . . . but the story wasn't even getting out of the gate. This happens. Like, all the time.

We talked before about the joy of getting lost in a story—finding a character you want to follow around, creating a world that you want to live inside—but the flipside of that pleasure is the discomfort that can come from total confusion. Especially when you're starting a new piece of writing, it's easy to feel intimidated: you're making the map at the exact same time as you're venturing into the territory.

Even people who've been writing for decades still have trouble finding their way into a new story and getting over that initial angst. After a few drinks, most writers will confess that they never really learn how to write in general—they just figure out how to accomplish *this* particular piece of writing, mostly by trial and painful error.

When you're writing a first draft, everything is up for grabs—and the ground is likely to shift under your feet as you make (and unmake) decisions. You're bound to keep changing your mind about your story's characters and premise and setting, and the whole thing will feel rickety af.

Especially during a scary bad time, when *nothing* in the real world makes any damn sense, and the facts keep shifting every day—it can be really frustrating to work on a story that also doesn't make sense and contains unstable information.

As far as I know, there's no way to avoid that sense of confusion and doubt—but it's possible to get used to it, and even comfortable with it. And even though this feeling isn't as pleasant as falling in love with your characters and worlds, I really believe that being okay with some creative unsteadiness can help you to cope with being alive in a rotten time.

Mental gymnastics

In the intro to this essay collection, I talked about how when you write your own story, you get to control every aspect—that's true, and we'll get more into it in the final section. But the truth is, writing is slippery, and control is often illusory. Your mind is a machine for rendering reality, but it's full of bugs and glitches that tend to jank everything up.

When you try to create a story that makes sense (in a way that reality often doesn't), you're going to end up doing a lot of mental gymnastics—and like real gymnastics, they will help you become more flexible in general. You can figure out the ways you're likely to screw up as a writer, and maybe screw up a little better. Plus you might get to glimpse the ways that your particular brain is a little wonky at turning blobs of information and sensory detail into a smooth narrative, which in turn can help you troubleshoot when the real world gets glitchy. (Is it your brain? Is it the outside world? Probably both. But it's helpful to have some sense of the exact ratio of each.)

Or to put it another way, when you write a story, you have to deal with a lot of uncertainty, which might just make you a little more able to deal with uncertainty in the real world. The hero of your story rides a flying motorcycle—no wait, the motorcycle can't fly, because then she could just zoom over the top of that barricade. Also, maybe she doesn't ride the motorcycle—maybe it's her friend's bike and she sits in a little sidecar. Or maybe the motorcycle is a unicycle? Also, what if she has a giant head and they don't make a helmet that size? And so on.

Even when the facts of your story are set in stone and you have a detailed outline, there's always the question of what to include and what to leave out, and how you're going to launch this story into motion. It can be fun to mess around with different scenarios, but it can also be pretty demoralizing to feel as though you can't get any traction.

I often find the process of starting a new piece of creative writing goes like this:

1. Whee a whole new world—let's find some cool image or idea to throw out there and see where it goes! So exciting much potential yayyyyy
2. Aaaaa what happened??? I'm stuck—why is everything going backward instead of forward? Where's my laudanum I must retire to my daybed bring my fainting couch I hate this
3. Oh wait, what if I . . . This could work! This could . . . Ugh. No. This didn't work
4. These characters have been sitting and drinking tea for five pages and I've run out of ways to describe the flavor of Lapsang souchong and nothing is happening send help!!!

When I was starting out and wrote dozens of short stories, I would try to get around this problem by introducing a conflict or central idea right in the opening sentence. Like, "The phoenix egg finally started to hatch, but my space cruiser was only three minutes away from blowing up." Like doing a cannonball into the freezing water, sort of.

I found that the more of a *situation* I could cram into those opening words, the greater the sense of momentum I could create, that could carry me through the rest of the story. (And then I had to go and fill in motivation, backstory, world-building, etc., as the intrepid hero was rushing to get the baby phoenix into an incubator, and off the exploding starship.) I still use that approach sometimes; it's how my story "Six Months, Three Days" begins, for example.

But that's just one workaround, and over time I found that it created some problems—like, sometimes the situation needs to build up more slowly, or be less clear-cut. And you might not want all of your stories to begin the exact same way. Plus of course, this doesn't at all solve the problem of "oh, actually, the motorcycle doesn't fly after all."

So the long-term solution is to just get used to the assembling-an-IKEA-bookshelf wobbliness when you start something. I usually feel like that pain is worth it, because you end up with something that's realer, or at least more interesting, than what you started out with.

You can never really control what your story is about, and that's exciting as well as scary. You can keep getting deeper into your mythos or finding a better conflict than the one you thought you had. That exploding-spaceship story could just be about saving the baby phoenix—or it could be about not feeling ready to become a parent to a magical space bird. Or maybe you realize that the baby phoenix actually *wants* to get blown up, so it can come back more powerful. Maybe the phoenix is carnivorous and wants to eat the main character. There are more ways this story could go than your bird has feathers.

This can be exhilarating as well as nerve-wracking, if you can learn to revel in the mercurial wildness of your own storytelling.

Promises you make to the reader are also promises to yourself

So your brain is a faulty machine for rendering reality—but then you're also creating something that might end up being loaded on other people's faulty brains.

I find it really helpful to have an imaginary reader in my head as I write. This is not the same person as your "inner critic"—that voice that tells you everything you're writing is garbage and you should quit now. Your inner critic is a manifestation of imposter syndrome, like we talked about in the previous chapter. But your imaginary reader is picking up what you're putting down. Sometimes literally.

Basically, your inner critic is a jerk whose negativity gets in the way of your process, but your inner reader is curious and delighted, and wants to know what's coming next. You should tell your inner critic to go screw themselves, but your inner reader can pull up a chair.

You can imagine surprising and delighting this nonexistent other person with all the funny dialogue and startling turns of events you're throwing into your story. Sometimes, it's easier and more fun to tell a story when you have a sense of who you're telling the story *to*. Especially if you're from a marginalized community, thinking of yourself as writing a story to, and for, other members of your community can keep you from worrying nonstop about what so-called "mainstream" readers will think.

Keeping an ideal reader in your mind helps you think about the promises you're making in the text, in the form of hints,

WHAT TO DO WHEN YOUR STORY WANDERS OFF COURSE

You set out to write a story about a man who's in love with his own clone, but somewhere along the way you ended up writing dozens of pages about the bakery where the clone buys scones. Soon, you have a story about a bakery, where the man and his clone are minor characters. Is this a problem?

Probably not. A lot of the fun of this racket is surprising yourself with unexpected discoveries, after all. Maybe the bakery just turned out to be more interesting than the clone romance, and you stumbled onto a story you really wanted to tell. It's like I said earlier: you could get bored with the ostensible protagonist of your story and realize some minor character is way more fascinating.

When I *have* had problems with lurching down the wrong path, it's usually been for a few reasons:

clues, dangling plot threads, foreshadowing, and so on. If I mention in the third sentence of a story that the main character has a nemesis with a chainsaw neck, who tends to turn up at the worst possible moments, then it's like a little Post-it Note reminding the reader that a chainsaw-necked fiend ought to show up later in the story. (And they're going to be in a really bad mood, because having a chainsaw for a neck tends to give you a nasty headache.)

Any promises you make to your reader are also promises that you're making to yourself. The knowledge that you left a shoe hovering in midair can motivate you to keep writing, because you have to get to the place where it drops.

Of course, you don't have to share your writing with any real-life humans, unless you want to. But even if you're the only person who ever reads your work, you can still have an imaginary reader in your head.

I only made it through writing *All the Birds in the Sky* by having a constant running dialogue with the reader in my head, who wanted to know what all this magic-and-science fuss was about. That weird question Patricia gets asked in the first chapter? Can't forget about that. The supercomputer in Laurence's bedroom closet? Probably gonna be something. In earlier drafts of the book, Laurence starts out by meeting some aliens who are operating out of a store called Jodhpurs & Jodhpurs, which only sells lentils and riding pants. And these aliens hint at huge secrets, which I figured I would pay off later. (The riddle and the supercomputer stayed, but the alien shopkeepers had to go.)

Even when my fiction was appearing in smaller markets and I wasn't getting much feedback from flesh-and-blood readers, I still kept an ideal reader in my head. I felt like I was in dialogue with this fake person. And as much as your characters can be your imaginary friends, I feel like the reader in your head can be one, too. And they can be a huge help when you're in the trudging-through-squelchy-mud period of starting a new story.

The whole time I was working on *All the Birds in the Sky*, I felt like I was making a bargain with that inner reader—please hang with me while I throw in a bunch of witchy stuff and gadgets and assassins and

1. I didn't start writing about the bakery because I was fascinated by the bakery, but because I didn't know where the romance should go next and I was stalling. Or I knew deep down that something intense needed to happen in the clone storyline, and I was instinctively shying away from it. The bakery was a delaying tactic.

2. The bakery story was me regurgitating clichés from other stories, going through the motions instead of moving forward. In this case, substitute something like "heist sequence" or "endless chase scene" for "bakery story." I was filling pages with stock events that didn't tell the story I wanted to tell.

3. I actually *was* more interested in the bakery than in the "likes attract" love story, but I couldn't admit it to myself. So I ended up with a hybrid monstrosity that still had the decaying flesh of my original idea clinging to it.

4. The conflict or stakes of the story became unclear, maybe because I got muddled in my

own head, or I kept changing my mind. Or worse yet, I set up huge stakes and then undermined them by giving the characters a get-out-of-trouble-free card with no spending limit.

So if you find yourself drifting way off the path you thought you were going down, it's probably fine. But you'll have to fully commit to this new direction. That means making sure that you're not just drifting off course out of inertia, and that those cupcake-frosting scenes really do live in your heart and mind on their own merits.

other weird ideas, and in return I will keep this story focused tightly on these two characters and their relationship. For every wacky plot device, there will be a couple pages of emotional, personal, grounded stuff. I felt like that awareness of a potential reader helped keep me on track, because I felt like I was holding someone's hand.

My own personal inner reader is kind of a cranky obnoxious weirdo who asks too many inappropriate questions, but it's nice to have someone to talk to while I write.

So when I'm scrabbling for purchase on the edge of a brand-new piece of fiction, and I have no idea what I'm doing, I try to focus on the little details about the characters and the world, for clues about where things should go next. I pretend I'm the reader as well as the writer, and focus on what the text thus far is telling me. And sometimes I will throw out way too many promissory notes, like a drunken prospector at closing time, in the hope that some of them will pay off. Like the late, lamented Jodhpurs & Jodhpurs.

I feel like most of us have no idea what we're doing most of the time, in life as well as in writing, but we're supposed to pretend we do. That's one reason for imposter syndrome, in fact. And for various reasons, it's sometimes easier to keep up that pretense when you're in the middle, or better yet the home stretch, of a story that's holding together somewhat. Starting a new work of fiction is scary precisely because you're at your most exposed—but you also have nothing to lose, in terms of this particular work at least.

Basically? Writing is one of the few areas where getting lost and confused can be liberating as well as terrifying. "No clue" can also mean "no fucks given."

CHAPTER 5

Everything Is Broken!
What Should I Write About?

Back in 2001, I was going through two huge changes. I was start-ing to transition seriously from male to female—and I was also becoming a novelist, after a few years of writing short stories.

I started out writing a novel based on my own experience of singing in church choirs as a kid. *Choir Boy* slowly morphed into a gonzo trans coming-of-age story that ruminated on mu-sic, the interplay between the sacred and the secular, the uses of beauty, and how we sometimes discover our true selves by pure accident. I was just finishing up my first draft of this novel in September 2001, when *you know what* happened. And then, I was convinced that nobody, absolutely nobody, was going to need a surreal weirdfest about gender fluidity and choral music anymore.

We were being dragged into war, Islamophobia was becom-ing government policy, and Brown people were being denied their civil rights. Everyone was scrambling to figure out how to respond to the USA PATRIOT Act and so much else. I felt utterly helpless, sitting in a cafe with a blank notebook and an EzGrip pen, wrestling with the ending to my novel while my friends were out mobilizing and actually making a difference.

Who the hell did I think I was, writing personal stories about the quest for an authentic self, during a time of war and atrocity?

Obviously I should change gears and start writing war novels. Or stories about fascism. I managed to finish *Choir Boy* and start the long journey to publication, but I also tried to speak to the terrifying moment we were living through. I wrote dozens of not-particularly-good meditations on state-sanctioned violence—most of which were a total waste of words, but one of which morphed, years later, into my novella *Rock Manning Goes for Broke*.

Eventually, though, a few things became obvious to me: 1) I had a lot of stuff to work out about gender and sexuality in my writing, and this was valid and important. 2) A moment of nationalist paranoia is exactly the time when we need more stories about being true to ourselves, at any cost. 3) I had a choice between writing pretty terrible war fiction and somewhat less terrible queer lit, and only one of those things was going to make me happy and leave me with the energy to do actual useful work in the world.

And I honestly don't think I could have made it through the early 2000s without all the brave queer voices I was reading and listening to. I went to a million open mics and book launches, and trans spoken word events, and every show felt like going to church. We were all figuring out this shit together, and we were carving out a space big enough to let us all grow and transform and change our minds.

When *Choir Boy* finally came out in the mid-2000s, I helped to organize a national tour with a group of trans authors and zinesters. All over the country, I found myself talking to trans and gender-nonconforming people who desperately needed to see ourselves reflected in fiction, so we could define what was possible for ourselves. We all needed each other's stories.

Write whatever you need to survive

When the whole world is on fire and the people you love are at risk, what should you write about?

Whatever you feel able to write. Whatever will make you

feel like you can keep living and fighting. Write the thing that you're ready and excited to write—not the thing that you feel the moment calls for, or the story that you think will fix every broken thing in the world. Your job is to survive, and maybe to help others to survive. That's it. That's more than plenty.

The past few years, I've had the same conversation a bunch of times, with other authors who couldn't write what they were "supposed" to be writing. Maybe they were trying to finish a serious, intense military fantasy book, but they kept "cheating" and writing a fluffy rom-com about magical chipmunk princesses in love. Or maybe they were trying to write something light and escapist, to get their mind off current events, but all that came out was a dark reflection of our real-life nightmares.

I want to unpack that idea of the thing you're "supposed" to write a little more, because it's super unhelpful. Maybe it comes from feeling obligated to speak to a particular historical moment, the way I did after 9/11, or maybe it comes from imposter syndrome and feeling like your stories aren't worthy. Or maybe you just really, really want to be "taken seriously," or break into the "mainstream." Whatever the reason, if you let all these expectations, real or imagined, keep you from writing whatever you feel drawn to, then you've already lost something unimaginably precious.

I also want to take the phrase "identity politics" and throw it into the sun. Because you know what? All politics is identity politics, because it's about who we are and who we want to be and who gets to have access to resources. Politics is nothing but the sum of our experiences, which include culture, gender, religion, sexuality, and disability. If we can't bring all of ourselves to the political sphere, then any struggle we take part in is already compromised.

Of course, there are times when you might need to write a particular thing—like, if you signed a contract in blood, or if it's an assignment for school, or if you promised your friends you'd finish a particular fanfic. But most of the time, it's not worth psyching yourself out, just so you can write the thing that you think someone else is expecting.

Just hearing your own thoughts over the shrilling of the atrocity organ can be a major challenge, especially when there's violence in your own streets. But making up your own stories about the world is a form of self-care and self-care is an important part of resistance. Plus we're going to need new writing, all kinds of new writing, and you never know which stories will end up being treasured, in ways that you could never predict. Storytelling is an important piece of protective equipment, even "frivolous" storytelling.

It's become sort of a cliché to say that you should write the book you wish you could read—but it's really true, and it's even truer during those times when the sky starts to melt. If there's a book that would comfort or distract or empower you right now, then you might need to be the one to write it. (And see the final essay of this collection for more about writing the book that only <u>you</u> could have written.)

There's no escape from writing about politics anyway

We're all trapped inside history and we can't see the outlines from where we are.

Wars, plagues, disasters, and struggles against tyranny come out of nowhere, and they can change the course of your whole life. This sucks: you're supposed to be the protagonist of your own damn story, but sometimes you're at the mercy of decisions made by politicians, cops, civic leaders, and cellophane dictators.

As we've discussed before, writing stories can be one way to make sense of the huge events you're caught in the middle of. So you might easily assume that the best way to deal with massive situations that are (mostly) beyond your control is to write about them, or to write about stuff like them. And sometimes, that approach does pan out—like in January 2017, when I put all my anxieties as a trans person into a story.

Still, one good thing about being trapped inside the belly of history is you can't avoid writing about it, no matter what. Sometimes the easiest way to cope with a situation is to write about something that seems unrelated—because really, everything is related in the end. You won't be able to keep reality from seeping into your work, no matter what you do, and every piece of storytelling is about politics, one way or another.

We'll talk more about finding story ideas in the next chapter, but for now, it's helpful to just let go of any worries about finding the "right" way to deal with a national (or global) shitshow in your fiction. If everything is messed up, then anything you write will end up touching on the messed-up stuff. Sometimes you can only see a systemic injustice from a great height, where you can look down and see the whole shape of it—but sometimes, you can only see it out of the corner of your eye.

A lighthearted romance between an elk princess and a swamp god might be the only thing you feel like writing these days—but it might also be the best way for you to deal with the problems everyone is facing.

Also, the stuff you want to write is probably pretty similar to whatever you feel drawn to read right now. If you're reading nothing but cozy mysteries, maybe you should try writing a cozy mystery. You can always think about your friends and loved ones, and what you think they might want to read right now—but don't get psyched out by trying to write something that's not for you, just to make someone else happy. Most of all, accept that you might need to be okay with changing gears on the regular, because the thing you feel like working on today might not be the same thing that feels good tomorrow.

Your daydreams could change the world

It's natural to fantasize when things are messed up, and sometimes those fantasies can turn out to be gold. Just look at those poor immigrant Jewish kids on the eve of World War II, who channeled all their longing to be powerful and safe into creating Superman and Batman. So many of our most beloved stories are just the craving of a powerless person for a way to imagine being powerful.

I used to long for a spaceship to swoop down and take me away from this horrendous planet, the way Yondu took Peter Quill away in *Guardians of the Galaxy*. The more terrified and anxious I get, looking at the state of the world, the more I take refuge in that daydream and mine it, endlessly, for more stories (like my recent young adult space fantasy *Victories Greater Than Death*).

You're under no obligation to be virtuous or high-minded—if you want to write a revenge fantasy about getting even with the jerkbags in charge, then go for it. Maybe you'll find that after a dozen pages, it turns into something else, or develops more layers. But if it just stays a pure revenge fantasy, that's awesome, too. Make it as gruesome as it needs to be.

That weird thought that keeps lodging in your mind in the shower? Turn it into a plot point.

That one time in your life when you felt really free, accountable to no authority figure or petty judge? Find a narrative thread about what someone could do with that much freedom.

That angry rant that you've been biting your tongue to keep from spouting on the sidewalk or the subway? Put a version of it in the mouth of a character, and then see what it spurs them to do next.

The best thing to write during a slow-motion tragedy is the thing that strengthens and amplifies your own perspective. Because there's nothing more badass and defiant than insisting that your stories matter, and that your experiences and concerns are important. In the end, that's how we make it to the other side: by bringing all of ourselves into our writing.

SECTION II

WHAT'S A STORY, AND HOW DO YOU FIND ONE?

CHAPTER 6

Don't Be Afraid to Go on Lots of First Dates with Story Ideas

A major source of shame and anxiety for writers, especially newer writers, is the "failure" to finish a story. What if you start a dozen stories and never quite find your way to the end of them? This might seem like a lack of follow-through, or even a reason to beat yourself up.

But maybe don't think of it as "failing" to complete something. Instead, try thinking of it as going on a bunch of blind dates—that don't happen to lead to second dates. No harm, no foul.

It's easy to get infatuated with a brand-new story idea. Check out that sexy elevator pitch, and all of those dazzling implications. This story idea is both rich and beautiful, and you want to get to know it a *lot* better. But then you spend a little more time together, and . . . the chemistry just isn't there. Turns out that elevator pitch only lasted a few floors, and all the implications just aren't panning out.

So just like with all the attractive singles in your area on every dating app, you might need to have one glass of merlot at a lot of wine bars before you find the premise you're ready to hang with.

There's no shame whatsoever in writing five sentences (or five pages) of a story before deciding that it's not going to click after all—you'll know you've found "the one" when it keeps popping into your head, and you keep thinking of more places you could go with it. Plus, sometimes you'll come back to one of those stories you started, and suddenly have a great idea of how to finish it. I've put plenty of half-finished stories aside, only to come back years later and find my way to the end of them.

I'm a stubborn cuss, so I have a hard time admitting that something isn't working and it's time to try something else. I used to try and force myself to keep going.

But lately, I've been realizing that I haven't actually gotten any better at finishing the stories I start. Instead, I've just gotten quicker to realize that something's not panning out, and it's time to jump tracks. When I was putting together my upcoming short story collection, I went back and looked through all the stories I wrote when I was starting out—and somehow, I had forgotten that for every story I finished, there were five or six that I didn't. And I found piles of notes and other evidence of me banging my head against the same wall over and over.

I had to learn to stop thinking of an unfinished story as an admission of defeat. To give myself permission to move on.

Of course, sometimes there's a story idea that I *know* in my bones is worth the effort, and I keep getting pulled back to it even though I can't bring it to life. That definitely happens on a semi-regular basis, and we'll talk in later chapters about how to deal with getting stuck when a story is both compelling and not working. But most of the time, I've found putting a story on the back burner is the right choice—my subconscious can keep poking at it, while I do other stuff. (And if I stop thinking about it at all, there's a sign that this was not meant to be.)

Another important lesson I had to learn: there's never any shortage of story ideas. They're easy to come by, and there's no need for a mindset of scarcity. If you think of story ideas as abundant, leaving stories unfinished will feel a lot less wasteful, and more like writing exercises, or good practice.

To return to the dating metaphor, you don't just want to find *a* story idea. You want to find *the* story idea that you're going to want to commit to. And there really are plenty of fish in the sea.

Why is it so hard to believe that story ideas are easy to come by?

Story ideas can feel magical, even miraculous. This is part of the mystique of writing, in fact. We're all used to falling in love with books based on the two sentences on the back cover, and the right idea, in the right hands, can feel electrifying. It's easy to believe that ideas are the key ingredient of great storytelling.

And yet, when you recognize that ideas are endless and bountiful, you won't just feel more relaxed about trying them out—you might also have an easier time coming up with new ones. Instead of being precious about any one idea, you can just keep brainstorming until you have a bunch that you like.

The universe contains a billion layers of miracles, outrages, and strange phenomena, and if everybody on Earth wrote one story per day for the next hundred years, we'd barely tap a tiny fraction of that potential. Every subgenre and plot device has a limitless number of stories that have never been written—like a playground that goes on and on forever. Every issue of *New Scientist* contains a ton of science-fiction story ideas, and you can get plenty of ideas from just taking a walk and people-watching (don't be creepy). Try to imagine one thing in the world changing drastically, or the weirdest thing that could happen to someone. Or get into a fight with a dead author, who won't mind at all.

Part of the fun of writing science fiction and fantasy is that there are almost no limits. If you're writing a murder mystery, you start out with the idea that someone is getting murdered, and the murderer will (probably) get caught. If you're writing a romance, two or more people are probably going to fall in love. SF and fantasy contain hundreds of subgenres, in which certain things are probably inevitable, like a steampunk story probably needs to blow off some steam. But still, when you start writing a piece of speculative fiction, that blank page can turn into almost anything you want.

Sometimes, a good story can start with a "what if," like: "What if vampires craved wizard blood?" Or a character who feels so compelling that you just want to follow them around, as we discussed previously. Or a world that you're dying to tell stories in. Or a particular setting that seems rich, like an old church or a generation ship. You could even start out with one particular scene that just needs to happen, and then the story grows around that one scene.

That's the wonderful thing about stories, really. Any part of the puzzle can be the first piece. (But just like with any puzzle, you can't move forward until you find the connections between the different pieces.)

What's the difference between a premise and a story?

Story ideas aren't just a never-ending bounty, they're also free (in the sense that nobody can own them). If a thousand writers all tackled the exact same idea at the same time, you'd end up with a thousand totally different stories—because what really matters, the hard part, is turning a premise into a story.

Like, take our vampires who only want to drink wizard blood. You could tell the story of a wizard who's on the run from hungry vampires. Or a vampire who's forced to drink the blood of the wizard who healed her mother. You could tell the story of the last remaining wizards on Earth, and their final desperate stand against the vampire army. Or the reluctant vampire-wizard alliance against their common enemy, the anemia pixies.

A good premise can go in any number of directions, and until you pick one of those directions, you don't really have anything. That process of turning a neato idea into a proper, full-fledged story isn't just about choosing a path—it's about everything from compelling characters, to lived-in world-building, to the hundreds of tiny details that turn a sterile idea-particle into a living, blooming, pollenating garden.

Put another way, "centaur bounty hunters" is a premise. "Centaur bounty hunters in love" is a story. "Centaur bounty hunters in love, but only one of them wants to capture the naiad alive" is an idea with legs. (No pun intended.)

So how can you tell if a story idea is worth your valuable time and attention? By trying to make it work. There's no diagnostic as useful as just trying to do the thing—and being okay with deciding at some point that it's not happening with this particular premise.

Perversely, I've often found that the more intriguing an idea is on the surface, the less likely it is to work for me. My hard drive is full of ideas that would make my ears prick up if I heard that someone else had written them—but they're just not going anywhere interesting for me. Often, the more basic an idea is, the greater the opportunity to find my own random spin on it, whereas the cleverest ideas tend to peter out. Maybe something about the process of grappling with a concept, shaking it down until something interesting rolls out, is essential to my creative investment.

And maybe this is because the ideas that look coolest on the surface are also the ones that have the most clear-cut implications. Whereas, if it's not immediately obvious who should be the protagonist, or how the conflict should play out, then I get intrigued and want to keep poking at it. Plus if I'm dead certain about what's going on in a story, before I even start writing, then I'm not going to be as fired up—because to me, part of the joy of writing is teasing out what's really happening, and what's really at stake.

To return to the dating metaphor, you start trying to get to know a potential story from the first moment you "meet." And just like in dating, it's impossible to separate those two processes: learning more, and figuring out if this is going to work or not. Your storytelling gears start turning, even as you try to see if this is the right match. How big a commitment are we talking here: a short story, a novella, a novel—or maybe just a piece of flash fiction? Is this something that's going to keep surprising and intriguing you, or are you going to feel like you're going through the motions?

I don't want to run that metaphor into the ground—but on a good day, starting to work on a story really is a lot like falling in love. Frustrating, anxiety-provoking, confusing, a cauldron of pure misery—and also, the best and most fulfilling thing ever. Most writing advice talks about mastery and "craft," the idea of imposing your will on a lump of unformed narrative. But my happiest writing times are usually when I'm seducing a story, and being seduced in turn.

And just like love, you'll know it when you see it. Love is patience, but love is also having the courage to ask for everything you need, and

A HUNDRED STORY IDEAS IN FIVE MINUTES

Lately, I've been speaking to high-school classes, and I have an exercise that I always get the students to take part in. I'll ask the students to suggest random items or concepts that a story could be about, like "potato" or "umbrella" or "running late."

Then we'll pick one of those, like "potato," and spend a few minutes coming up with twenty things that could happen to a potato. Maybe the potato gets married. Maybe it grows legs and learns to walk. Maybe the potato runs for president.

But that's just the premise. For each of those twenty things, we try to think about different ways to approach the story. In the story about a potato getting married, is the main character the potato? Or the person who gets married to the potato? Or the potato farmer? And we also come up with as many central conflicts as possible. Maybe someone has religious objections to potato marriage, or maybe there's no wedding ring that fits on a potato-finger. Finally, we try to dream up some complications, or unexpected turns, that the story could take.

At the end of five to ten minutes, we've usually come up with a hundred or so story ideas, and at least some of them feel like they could start sprouting some potato shoots.

not settle for less. You can tell when a story was written with love, versus when someone did their duty.

The only difference between love affairs and story writing? You probably can't put a potential romance on ice for a year or twelve and be certain that your date will still be excited to see you whenever you're ready to come back.

CHAPTER 7

The Secret to Storytelling? Just One Good Scene, and Then Another, and Another.

There's only one thing more intimidating than a blank first page, and that's a blank tenth page. At least when you are starting a new piece of writing from scratch, anything is possible. But once you've started weaving a bunch of narrative threads, you'll have a much harder time unweaving them.

So what do you do when you're struggling to find a way forward, in the middle of a piece of writing? There's no one answer, and we'll keep coming back to this question in later chapters. But one solution is just to try and write a good scene. And then write another one, until the scenes start to add up to something. A big part of writing any first draft is just seeing what works: how do these characters fit together, and what can we do with this premise and this setting? If you can get three halfway decent scenes in a row, then you're cooking: the characters click, the story takes shape.

The scene is the basic unit of storytelling, most of the time: one or more people, in a particular location (or set of locations), having some kind of interaction.

And each scene is a little story unto itself, in which the characters have a problem or a conflict, and they grapple with it. There are twists, and unforeseen developments, and revelations. Things may have gotten worse by the end of the scene—in fact, if this is the middle of the story, it's usually better if things don't get sorted too easily. And then the scene ends with some final moment: someone leaves, a gauntlet is thrown, the conflict intensifies, or maybe there's a final grace note that leaves us reflecting on what just happened.

And just like a whole story, as a general rule a good scene is one where something changes. Or at least, something *happens.* The thing that happens doesn't have to be huge: some of my favorite scenes are just people hanging out, arguing over lunch, or going clothes shopping. But if a scene is good, then things probably won't be exactly the same at the end as they were in the beginning.

Just to be clear: when I talk about a "good" scene, I don't mean a well-written one, or a polished one, or even one that you're sure belongs in this story. In this context, "good" means "interesting." A good scene leaves you wondering what's going to happen next, or more absorbed in the characters and their issues. A good scene should probably feel as if things are cooking, and like the story is going someplace, even if you don't yet know where.

Also, "good" doesn't mean "realistic." In real life, people take forever to get around to saying what's on their mind, and a lot of interactions are pointless or boring. Even the most literary piece of fiction, with the strongest commitment to realism, will edit stuff out, or streamline, or stylize. Just look at Dave Eggers' preface to *A Heartbreaking Work of Staggering Genius,* in which he explains that all the dialogue in his memoir has been rewritten, edited, and then rewritten a second time, to make the author and his friends sound less dorky.

And after watching approximately 10,000 hours of the CW, I've started to notice just how ruthlessly efficient the scenes in a typical episode of *The Vampire Diaries* or *Arrow* are. Each episode is juggling a dozen subplots, so every scene needs to carry its own weight and move at least one subplot forward, if not several. Characters on the CW enter each scene with an axe to grind, or a problem they need to solve, or often the need to murder each other. They interact, and something shifts in their dynamic, often heightening their conflict (if it's the middle of an episode), and then each scene ends with some kind of knife twist—or neck twist, if it's *Vampire Diaries*.

If you want to see how to strip a scene down to just its bones, then watching the CW provides a masterclass.

How to find a scene

Often a scene will start out with one of two needs: something needs to happen, or two or more characters need to talk about something.

In the first case, you might know what happens, but not how it happens. For example, Marjorie the dancing witch is supposed to leave home to search for the Lost Clogs of Basingstoke—but she could leave in a sweet tear-soaked farewell, or in a screaming rage. If the point is just to get Marjorie out the door and on the road, then you can accomplish that in a couple sentences. But you want this to be a moment that will stick in people's minds. And the better the send-off, the better you'll be able to stick with her on her long journey.

So I end up spending a lot of time thinking about the best way to dramatize an incident. The most boring version of the scene is easy to reach, because I've already seen it a million times. The more interesting version, the one that makes the characters feel real and compelling, often takes a lot of second-guessing.

To create a moment that feels coolest to me, I have to really put myself in the scene. And ask myself a million questions:

What is Marjorie thinking/feeling as the scene begins?

Did she already decide to leave home, or does she decide halfway through this interaction?

Does everyone else know she's going to leave, or is this a surprise to them?

If I know in advance that something needs to happen in a scene, then I try my best to make that action a surprise—or at least introduce some minor wrinkles. If Marjorie goes into the scene knowing she has to go on a clog-quest, then maybe she ought to be confronted with a surprising reason why she should stay at home. The best iteration of a scene is usually—not always—the one that generates the most conflict and suspense.

In the second case, sometimes you know that two characters need to have a conversation about an issue between them, which could be something that's happened, or something that one of them just learned about. This is my favorite thing in the world to write. I love complex worlds and plots and stuff, but my happiest writing times are always when I feel like two characters have something to say to each other.

Any interaction between two or more people is a conversation, really. A fight scene is a conversation, and so is a sex scene. I just love writing any kind of moment where relationships shift, someone's baggage gets unpacked and/or repacked, and conflicts are deepened. Perversely, the more action-oriented the scene, the more you might need to be aware of the emotional content and the POV, because the stakes are always at least somewhat personal, even if the fate of the world is at stake.

Sometimes I'll know that two characters can't really meet up and talk about their issues with each other for another hundred pages—but that's the scene I'm most excited to write, so I just go ahead and write it now. I'm a big believer in eating dessert first. I'll write whatever scenes I'm most stoked about writing, and worry later about putting them together in some kind of order. Sure, this gets me in trouble occasionally, but I get stuck slightly less often.

Again, "good" doesn't mean "polished." The first draft of any scene is bound to be clunky as hell. The characters will blurt out their innermost thoughts in a totally unrealistic fashion, or they'll speak the subtext out loud. People will often be way too easygoing, or they'll pick a fight for no reason at all. Conversations will feel lifeless, and people will make decisions that don't make sense in the moment.

But at least there'll be little moments here and there where people say something revealing, or their personalities shine through. And maybe I'll notice that Marjorie and her sister don't really get along, and that's a thread I can try and pick up again in later scenes. The bad version of a scene nearly always contains the seeds of a better version.

Another problem I run into pretty often: I'll have two or more scenes that cover the exact same ground. When I have a story that's too long or feels aimless, I usually find that redundant scenes are part of the problem—like, two characters have the identical conversation two or three different times, with minor variations. As soon as I merge those scenes into one, everything immediately flows way better.

Psyching yourself up

I don't always outline a story or a novel before I write, but I frequently find myself outlining a scene, beat by beat. Does it start in the middle, or do we follow a character into the scene? What are the bits that need to happen, and in what order? What's the through-line that carries us from the beginning of the scene to the end? A lot of making a scene work is a matter of psyching yourself up, and trying to figure out at least some idea of what's going on, even if the action ends up surprising you as you write it.

Here's a good place to introduce a couple of ideas that I'm going to keep coming back to:

1. Every writer is also an actor.

The process of getting inside the head of a character, figuring out their motivations and shouldering their baggage, is more or less the same for writers as for actors. (I was a failed actor in high school, and spent a fair amount of time learning to get into character before I realized I was just bad at it. I tried to imagine everything from the physical sensation of someone's worn-down shoes to the internal monologue that propels them on stage.)

You have to focus on trying to put yourself in the character's shoes until it becomes second nature and you start to know this person, inside and out. Sometimes, I'll act a tricky scene out—even doing the voices out loud in the shower. (I know, I know.)

2. Suspension of disbelief is just as important when you're writing as when you're reading—or maybe even more so.

A scene only works if you can convince yourself that it's real to the characters, and that the stakes *matter*. In his indispensable book *About Writing*, Samuel R. Delany says that when writers go back and change an event in their fiction, they have to "convince themselves that the story actually did happen . . . in the new way," and that the original version was hearsay, or a misunderstanding of the events.

In other words, you almost have to hypnotize yourself into thinking that the events you're writing about are real, and they actually took place.

So once I've got the basic elements of the scene down, then I go back and think about the details more carefully. Where does the scene take place? And what are the characters doing during the scene?

I'll frequently write a conversation between two or more people as if it takes place in a blank void at first. Then I'll stop and think, what's the most interesting location for this to happen? Are they eating lunch at a restaurant? Are they at fencing practice? Are they doing a spacewalk? It's more interesting to have a relationship conversation while flying over an active volcano than sitting in a Starbucks. And the same way that I often need something to do with my own hands when I talk, it's always better if the characters are doing something during an interaction, instead of just standing still.

I also try to make the scene-setting do actual work, conveying information or setting up stuff that's going to happen later. Or establishing a location that I'm going to keep reusing. (More on that in a later chapter.)

And speaking of suspense, a relatively quiet and benign conversation can take on an extra charge if the reader knows that a ten-ton kaiju is about to show up and stomp on the characters' house. These people are sitting there processing their feelings, and you're like, "Stop being introspective and get out of there before it's too late, you twerps!" It's also always fun to do a *Henry V*–style "little touch of Harry in the night" scene where various people have One Last Talk before the big battle. Or a whispered conference while sneaking into the villain's lair.

And once I know where the scene takes place and what else is happening, I'll often start a scene with the characters talking, and then do the scene-setting in the third or fourth paragraph, once we're already in the flow of events.

For my novel *All the Birds in the Sky,* I wrote tons of scenes, just trying to find the characters and their voices. My hard drive is full of documents with titles like "5000 words of Laurence and Patricia getting closer" and "5000 words of people trying to tear Patricia and Laurence apart," and "A series of emotional vignettes about Laurence and Patricia." I wrote scene after scene, and then only used a small fraction of the scenes I wrote.

All too often, the scenes that make me most excited about the story when I'm writing a first draft are the same ones that I end up having to cut in revision.

Before, we talked about how your characters can be your "imaginary friends." And to me, part of scenework is just hanging out with these friends I've created for myself. (As I mentioned earlier, I was a social outcast when I was a kid, and frequently wandered alone making up stories in my head.) The more time I spend taking my characters through different scenarios, the better I know them, and the more I can lose myself in their world.

CHAPTER 8

The Most Powerful Thing a Story Can Do Is Show How People Change

Fiction is superior to real life in one important respect: a story can show change happening in real time.

Over the course of a novel or short story, people open their hearts, or close them. Rulers fall, or ascend. People fall in love, and/or fall out of love. Parents and children reconcile. Empires are overthrown, oppressors are defeated, and mysteries are solved. Friendships are tested, and sometimes broken. Enemies become friends, and then lovers. Evil people realize the error of their ways, and good people realize that doing good isn't as simple as they believed.

In a made-up story, you can see justice taking shape—or being thwarted. You can show how the human heart struggles with huge questions, and sometimes even finds an answer.

In real life, meanwhile, people do change, but it takes too long and progress is always fragile. You only have to look at opinion surveys on anti-racism, police brutality, same-sex marriage, trans rights, immigration, and a host of other issues to see how people's views have changed in a relatively short time. But it can still be frustrating to fight and struggle and argue and wait for the battleship of public opinion to turn.

We're all at the mercy of Dornbusch's law: A crisis always takes much longer to arrive than you think it will, and then it always happens much faster than you expected.

Fiction allows us to skip over the excruciating, boring part where people are digging in their heels and the status quo appears unshakable. To distill those moments of transformation that are way too rare in real life down into a cocktail of pure, intoxicating flux. We don't just crave fiction because we want to escape reality—but because fiction contains the best and worst parts of reality, without all the middling garbage that pads it out.

Like I said in the first chapter (about imaginary friends), we care about characters who go through changes. A character who doesn't evolve is just a pet rock: fun to look at, but not super compelling. There are two major ways a character can change: their opinions and feelings can shift, or their circumstances can. Or both.

People often talk about characters having an "arc," which brings to mind the image of an arrow shot in the air, curving upward only to come down again. But another useful image is a piece of coal coming under immense pressure and becoming a diamond. People don't change when life is easy and straightforward—they change when life is a bloody confusing nightmare.

The hard part is making people believe in change

Because we all crave narratives of transformation, we actively root for characters to level up, or to come to their senses, or sometimes to take the plunge into doing cathartically terrible things. Reading the A Song of Ice and Fire books, I can't tell you how many times I shouted at the page, because I was ready for Sansa Stark to stop letting Petyr Baelish wrap her around his little finger. (And I've definitely heard from readers who felt frustrated at how long it took some of my own characters to wise up to something.)

And yet, a story still has to meet the reader halfway. When a character makes a huge change that seems to come out of nowhere, this is frustrating precisely *because* we've been rooting for that character to change. We can all think of stories where huge character moments felt unearned and unsupported by everything that came before. Case in point: when you watch classic *Doctor Who*, you can always tell a companion is about to leave the TARDIS when she conveniently falls in love with someone she's barely spoken to until five minutes ago (*cough*Leela*cough*).

Oftentimes, character growth comes down to one of the following:

- A character couldn't do a thing before, and now they can.
- Or they were not willing to do a thing before, but now they're willing.
- They've been wrestling with a choice, or a difficult relationship, and now they have clarity.
- Also on the relationship tip, two characters work out (some of) their issues with each other.
- An identity crisis, or a crisis of faith or ideology, has reached some resolution.

Any of those things can also happen in reverse: characters can become less able to do something they could do before, and they can lose clarity as well as gain it. Also, the above categories are very broad-brush by design, and definitely not intended to be exhaustive.

But if you think of your characters as gaining XP over the course of your story, then you're gonna want to make them work for it. Cheap epiphanies are worthless, and any problem or conflict that gets solved too easily probably wasn't that big a deal to begin with. Not that we need to see people suffer endlessly, but they at least need to wrestle with whatever dilemma they're facing.

The more major the characters, the more we need to see them earn any change of heart or status. For minor and/or supporting characters, we can assume they've done a lot of work while we weren't paying attention to them. It can actually be cool to catch up with a character we haven't seen for a hundred pages, and they've had some personality upgrades in the meantime.

In order to follow an arc, we need to have a clear sense of where a character starts out, what the character is struggling with, what exactly they're aware of, what their goals are, and the ways in which their struggle gets more complicated or more painful as the story goes on. One of my unpublished novels, a portal fantasy, suffered from some of this: I kept wavering on stuff like how much power my protagonist starts out with, and how much she already knows about magic, and what exactly her unresolved issues are. And the result was a messy arc that nobody could follow.

I always say, you can't twist the knife until you find the knife.

I often don't know what the big character turns in a story or novel are going to be until I've written a lot of it. Even if I outlined a ton in advance, the character stuff is usually the hardest to predict until I spend a lot of time with it. That's one reason why I try to write a bunch of interesting scenes: so I can see how the characters are changing, or could change, and write toward that. I'll inevitably write the beats out of order and skip over important bits, and then I try to create a coherent progression as I revise. But in the first draft, I still try to find the bones of the character arc as I write, because that's one of the best ways to find a satisfying ending.

What if your characters just refuse to change?

It's hard to invest in a character who never changes—though obviously not impossible, judging by the popularity of James

Bond and most iconic superheroes. But sometimes you reach the middle of a story and realize that your protagonist is just . . . stuck. You have a character who's going through the plot motions, but standing still in all the ways that matter.

This can happen for all sorts of reasons:

You might have picked the wrong person as a protagonist. I can't tell you how many times I started out building a story around someone who seemed, on paper, like the ideal main character—only to find them kind of lifeless. And meanwhile there was this other supposedly minor character who kept popping up here and there, and seemed to have a lot of issues they were anxious to come to terms with.

You've written a perfect human being instead of a flawed individual. This is easy to fall into, especially since you want your hero to be "likable," which can easily translate into "well-adjusted." But even if your character's arc isn't explicitly about overcoming a flaw, or learning to stop engaging in bad behavior, they're going to need some issues. Or they won't be real enough to change.

Nobody in your story is willing to call the hero on their shit. This is a similar problem. You want everyone else to love your main character as much as you do, so all the other characters in your story treat them as if they can do no wrong. No matter how selfishly or obnoxiously the hero behaves, they get a free pass, and thus they can never grow out of anything.

Your protagonist doesn't want anything. Every character needs goals or desires—and they don't have to be related to the plot. In fact, I often find that a character who's chasing after something unrelated to the search for a plot widget is more interesting. Years ago, I was writing a story about a man who gets arrested for copyright violation because he has a piece of music stuck in his head (and this is an unauthorized copy). The main character was just a cipher until I decided that he desperately wanted to take his sick dog to the vet—and this gave him a more specific and personal reason to want to get out of the gnarly situation he was in.

You just need to apply more pressure. See the "diamond" metaphor above. Sometimes a lifeless character just needs another element to make them uncomfortable. Maybe they need a nemesis whom they loathe (but will learn to love later). Or they're going to be forced to marry their own evil future self—I hate when that happens. It's amazing how often a character just needs a foil, or someone to bounce off, to start going through some changes.

Your ostensible protagonist isn't driving the action. As a general rule, the more a story is focused on plot widgets, the more your hero ought to be making stuff happen, rather than being a bystander. The concept of "agency" is very culturally loaded, and rooted in a lot of Eurocentric cis male notions of "rugged individualism"—but in a story about searching for the magic bidet of the Elf King, the hero should at least be trying to find that bidet. Someone who gets dragged along for the ride by other characters might end up having fewer opportunities for personal growth.

I'm a sucker for a story about someone who changes the world, and is changed in the process. In fact, I have a hard time believing in a person who travels through the Valley of Improbable Plumbing (searching for that magic bidet) and doesn't emerge with a new outlook on life. The more I feel trapped in situations that I seemingly have little or no control over, the more I want to write and read about people who take action. But this is only comforting if I believe in the journey, which in turn means the main character needs to be changed by their experiences.

Fiction can work all kinds of magic during horrendous times: inspire us to resist evil, expose the reality of the world, create empathy, and help us to understand complex systems from a vantage point that could be hard to reach in nonfiction. But the most powerful thing that fiction can do is show that people can change, and that we all have the potential to be different. That's where I get a lot of my hope when everything around me feels hopeless.

CHAPTER 9

A Good Plot Is Made Out of Two Things

Every plot can be boiled down to two basic elements: plot devices, and turning points. This is true whether the plot is "buying a hat" or "saving the world."

Like every other aspect of writing, plots tend to get pretty mystified, because when they actually work, they seem bigger and more magical. But plots are just mechanisms, made up of levers and cranks and pulleys, which give the characters a reason to move through the story. Plots are interesting if they're clever, or if they help the characters develop, or if they set up interesting situations.

But when a plot really clicks, the plot devices take on a whole other meaning and life of their own. It's like that stuffed animal that you got on a trip to the seaside arcade with your family: it's just a lump of stuffing and fake fur, with a crude cartoon face. But the longer it sits on your bedside table, the more it feels like an extension of the people you love, and the more emotion you put into it.

So what are these two elements?

A **plot device** is a thing, or an idea, or a contrivance, that creates conflict and forces the characters to take action. The characters have to achieve some goal, or they want to prevent something from happening, or they want to escape from a bad situation. Many plots boil down to "I want this sandwich, but someone else doesn't want me to have this sandwich."

Alfred Hitchcock popularized the term "McGuffin," meaning an object that everybody is searching for—like the Maltese

Falcon. Creators like Quentin Tarantino and J.J. Abrams have taken this concept to its ultimate extreme, building complex plots around McGuffins that we never learn much about. There's a mysterious briefcase, or a Sith dagger, and they're important mostly because they give the characters a reason to act, rather than because of anything intrinsically interesting about them.

But a plot device can also be something like "we're locked up in a space prison that's about to self-destruct, and the last escape pod launches in an hour," or "two bitter enemies must work together to solve a mystery." Plot devices frequently shade over into being tropes, something we'll talk about later.

And a **turning point** is just what it sounds like: a moment where everything changes, and the plot veers off on another trajectory. You can only follow one thread for so long before you need to switch things up. It can be useful to diagram your favorite movie or book and spot these inflection points—often, they come when a secret is revealed, a quest comes to an unfortunate end, a character dies, heroes suffer an unfortunate setback, or shit otherwise gets real.

Basically, if a given plot device starts wearing out its welcome, you can swap it out for another one (or a whole cluster of them). If the characters have spent a hundred pages trying to escape from a dungeon or pull off a heist, then the turning point comes when they either fail or succeed. And there are unforeseen consequences either way, which turn things sideways.

Did you ever find yourself standing in your kitchen, but you couldn't remember what you went in there to get? That's the way a lot of first drafts are, and it's actually fine. Your characters go to a place, for reasons, but you kept changing your mind about what those reasons were, or you actually forgot to give them a reason to go there. It's really fine.

Plot devices are the easiest things to add, or change, in revision. We get overly attached to them—because again, when they work, they seem magical. But in real life, we generally have five different reasons for everything we do. You might go to Pittsburgh to visit your uncle, but also there's a bookstore you've been dying to visit, and you'd like to be out of town when your ex is having a wedding. And it's shockingly easy to change "we had to sneak into the fortress to steal the secret plans" to "we had to sneak into the fortress to rescue somebody." Frequently, making such a seemingly major change means rewriting one exposition-filled scene, plus a line of dialogue here and there.

What people do is usually more interesting than *why* they do it—unless the "why" is really personal, and has to do with their character arcs. But if their actions are just about a widget, then the widget is pretty interchangeable. Until it isn't.

How, and when, to commit to plot devices

At a certain point, a plot device gets embedded in the foundation of your story. The characters start having emotional attachments to the McGuffin, and the themes and ideas of the narrative connect deeply to a particular thing or situation. And maybe the ending of the story really only works with one exact configuration of gears and turbines. You get enough connective tissue and these plot wingdings will start to feel significant.

At that point, you can no longer just change the reason for a major sequence of events, without tearing out lots and lots of drywall.

I try to hold off committing to plot devices until I get to the revision stage, because I'm always worried about the cart driving the horse. I've had plenty of occasions where my characters got twisted into knots trying to make a plot thing work, when

I only put the plot thing there in the first place to help the characters advance.

Sometimes, I'll throw in a dozen plot devices and see which one sticks—and by "sticks," I mean "generates some good moments and causes the characters to come alive." I will write a scene where the characters talk about some mysterious secret weapon or whatnot, and then I'll just find myself forgetting to mention the secret weapon again for another twenty or thirty pages, because the characters lost interest in it. Or really, *I* lost interest in it. My first drafts are littered with bits and bobs that seem super important, and then are never spoken of again.

For example, in my new young adult novel *Victories Greater Than Death*—minor spoiler alert—there's a plot device called the Talgan stone. Early drafts of the book had everybody searching for the long-lost Talgan stone, and it felt like too basic of a McGuffin. I was leery of writing scene after scene where people talked about the search for this doohickey, and I couldn't make up my mind about what this thing even was. So I dropped the Talgan stone like a hot rock and wrote three or four drafts without it.

Then, late in the revision process, I had to go back and find something to add a sense of momentum to the first half of the book. I needed an object that would get the characters where I wanted them to be at the midpoint of the book, and give them the information they needed. I racked my brain . . . and ended up finding the Talgan stone, right where I'd dropped it. And huzzah, it was exactly what I needed, because now I was clear on what I needed it to do.

And that's the crux: sometimes you have a plot device just to have a plot device, and it just ends up generating more clutter. And then sometimes, you have a yawning chasm in your story, or you need something to add stakes and tension early on, and a good plot device can be just the thing. And again, plot devices aren't just objects—they can be stuff like "we got locked in a cage" or "my evil brother-in-law just showed up."

It's tricky to generalize about plot devices, because different types of stories have different needs. Try to imagine if Douglas Adams was forced to include fewer random incidents and outlandish objects in his writing—it would be tragic. A spy thriller needs gadgets and ticking ticky things and villain lairs, or it's a total epic fail. And yet in many cases, less is more. Like, say, if you have a Sith dagger, you might not also need a Sith wayfinder, because those are basically the same thing twice. Just sayin'.

Time to blow up some dichotomies, because that's my brand

If you've ever read any of my fiction, you'll know that I love to smash false oppositions and binaries into tiny fragments of rhetorical schmutz.

So here are two dichotomies I want to take a sledgehammer to:

"Pantser vs. plotter": You'll hear this one a lot in writing things. Sometimes it's also described as "gardener vs. architect." The idea is that some writers just make everything up as they go along, without any idea of where the story might be going, and they sort of "discover" the plot as they go. And other writers will meticulously plan out every last bit of the story beforehand, and maybe even just expand that outline little by little, until it becomes a full draft.

The truth is, most writers do some of both. Even if you plan everything carefully, some stuff inevitably doesn't work and has to be rethought, and character stuff will often land differently than you expected. And even the most spontaneous writer will have some idea of where things are going, and will maybe make notes on what ought to be coming.

I've found every way there is to screw up writing a story.

My adult novels have tended to be more make-it-up-as-you-go, while my young adult trilogy has been pretty painstakingly outlined. I've also had the privilege of working in a couple of television writers' rooms, where we outlined the whole season, then each individual episode, then each individual scene. *So* many index cards. Because I'm a person writing about people, it's impossible to plan everything—but it's also impossible to get anywhere unless I'm making *some* plans and thinking ahead.

It's not an either/or, it's a spectrum. You never want to close yourself off to happy accidents, but you want to have some stuff up your sleeve no matter what. And you'll always have to rethink things in revision.

"Character-based vs. plot-based": This is a distinction I used to hear endlessly when I was starting out as a fiction writer. Supposedly, some stories are based more on characters and their emotional journeys, while others are purely about chases and fights and puzzles and ticky things. The former sort includes romances as well as literary works, while the latter category re-

WRITING EXERCISE: PRETEND YOU'RE WRITING THE SCRIPT FOR AN *ASTEROIDS* MOVIE

Asteroids was a video game back in the early 1980s, about a ship with one thruster and one gun, shooting at rocks in space. That's it. That's the whole concept.

Now imagine that you've been hired to write the screenplay for an *Asteroids* movie. You have the basic idea (pew-pew-pew rocks), but you have to fill in the gaps and create something with characters, and a plot that feels less repetitive than rock after rock. Who are the people inside this ship? Why are they trapped in the middle of nowhere, blasting space junk? What do they want, besides not getting smashed to pieces?

Asteroids: The Movie could be a number of different genres. It could be a romance about two or more people who come together to survive an endless jagged onslaught. Or a dystopian story about rebelling against the corporation, or government, that trapped these people in a bad situation. You could turn it into a disaster movie, or a psychological thriller about people losing their shit in space. There could be a terrorist who's using asteroids as weapons.

Most importantly, *Asteroids: The Movie* needs to be a story about people, in which the personalities and goals on board that tiny vessel become the drivers of the plot.

So try and figure out what genre you'd want to make *Asteroids* into—and then think of a reason why your characters are in this situation. A plot device that strands them on this one-gun ship. And then come up with three turning points that could happen, that would change their status quo and move the story into a new phase. Write a one-paragraph synopsis of the first two-thirds of *Asteroids: The Movie* (feel free to pick a different game), with a clear setup and easy-to-spot inflection points. Get ready to (space) rock!

fers to spy stories, action-adventures, political thrillers, and romps.

Once again, I'd say this is a spectrum rather than an on-off switch. Almost every story is some mix of character stuff and plot stuff, and the mix can vary from page to page and chapter to chapter. Character *is* action: people aren't just a collection of feelings and opinions and habits, but rather the sum total of all the choices they take. Meanwhile, even the plottiest plotfest needs to have characters who we root for, or else none of the secret codes and countdowns will matter worth a damn.

Both of these binaries are worth questioning, because creating a good plot might require you to be able to change modes again and again. Sometimes you need to take a step back and do more planning, while at other times you might need to blow up everything and just make things up as you go along. Sometimes a plot device isn't working because the characters aren't invested enough in it, which in turn is because you're not invested enough in the characters.

And sometimes your characters are lifeless because the plot isn't generating enough urgency. It's a freaking ecosystem, people.

The downside of describing a plot in mechanistic terms, as I've done above, is that you might start to think of a steady-state machine, which just chugs along at a constant pace until it finally shuts down. Plots, meanwhile, need to pick up their pace and urgency and intensity as they go along, so they can reach some kind of crescendo toward the end. To raise the stakes, you have to earn the reader's (and your own) trust and suspension of disbelief—if we're not fully convinced that one giant rock-tunneling spider is bad, then we won't be scared when there's suddenly an army of giant rock-tunneling spiders.

So if your plot is a machine, it's a rocket: it needs to keep accelerating in order to achieve escape velocity. And it needs to keep the people inside it alive, rather than letting that acceleration smush them to death.

*

CHAPTER 10

How to Tell a Thrilling Story
Without Breaking Your Own Heart

"Things get worse."

That's the closest there is to a formula for generating excitement in a story. It's also a pretty good description of the real world, when plagues and disasters and political crises start compounding each other.

Once you've got a decent plot, most writing advice will tell you to keep turning up the heat on your protagonist(s), with some shocking events, or major setbacks, that'll make your characters miserable. And sure, it's important to have a sense of "rising action" so that your story can reach some kind of peak before the conflict is resolved—but when you're writing during a time when history is getting all histrionic (which is what this book is about, after all), then you *might* need to take it a little easier on yourself.

It's not at all true that horrible things need to happen to your characters, to move your story forward. Quite the opposite—there are plenty of other ways to add urgency or momentum. There's no need to risk traumatizing yourself (or your eventual reader) just to make things more challenging for your characters.

This could be one reason why it's so much harder for many of us to do creative writing when the whole world turns into stinktown. Bad news is impossible to escape, and meanwhile everything bad that happens in fiction reminds us of the horrendous real world. Of course, writing scary stuff could be cathartic, the same way that eating spicy food cools you off during hot weather. But if you find it too upsetting to write atrocities, then . . . don't.

Especially in a first draft, it's pretty normal to feel like you're pulling your punches, even at the best of times. I often get to the middle of a draft and realize that things are too easy for the characters, or certain incidents could stand to be more hair-raising. But the opposite happens just as often: I'll realize that I went overboard with a nasty turn of events, and I don't need to have a truck run over the main character's dog on the same day that her house burns down. No matter what, you're always going to find yourself dialing the nastiness up or down in revision—so there's no point in making things horrible for horribleness' sake in the first draft.

You can always get that same sense of rising action and increased stakes by having your characters make some questionable decisions—or try to fix their problems, only to make them worse. There's no need to make yourself sad or upset, dreaming up an ordeal for your characters to go through, when you can dwell on what your characters know, and what options they have at this point in the story. Not only do active characters make for better storytelling most of the time, but it can be downright therapeutic to make your protagonists the (inept, fumbling) masters of their own fate.

And paradoxically, it's often a bigger gut punch when people bring disaster on themselves instead of just getting sideswiped by some external force.

Meanwhile, when you do write about horrific events, it's important to think about trauma—both the causes and the consequences of it. Atrocities aren't just a plot device, they're an opportunity to look at the reasons why abusive systems exist, and also the lasting ways that they affect people.

Raising the stakes without undercutting your characters

Pain and cruelty are just like any other story element: they're tools. You use them to get the effect you want, and if they're not useful, you can cast them aside without a second thought.

In a few drafts of my novel *The City in the Middle of the Night*, Bianca visits the bandit city of Argelo, where she revels in her newfound freedom. She parties way too hard, until she passes out from booze, drugs, and sleep deprivation—and then someone tries to rape her. Sophie rescues Bianca while this man is still taking her clothes off, and knocks him out cold. But Bianca soon realizes that her would-be rapist is a leader of one of the city's ruling families, and as soon as he wakes up, Sophie and Bianca will be put to death for hitting him in the head. So the two women have no choice but to make sure this dude never wakes up again, and then they have to find a way to dispose of the body, which leads to more complications.

This sequence raised the stakes and created a greater sense of menace, but I started to have three a.m. arguments with myself about using an attempted rape as a plot device. I didn't want to trivialize rape, and I definitely didn't want to include sexual assault if I wasn't going to be able to deal thoughtfully with the aftermath. But just as important, I didn't want to create the impression that the bad choices Bianca makes later in the story are a result of sexual assault, rather than her own personal shortcomings.

I struggled with this for a long time—longer than I should have, in retrospect. As soon as the assault was gone from the story, I could see clearly that *The City in the Middle of the Night* was better without it.

As traumas go, sexual assault is massively overused, and it's too often a pat motivation for characters to go off the rails. Fictional sexual violence can re-traumatize survivors, and too often it's thrown into a story without paying attention to the ways it affects someone's life afterward. The media often presents sexual assault according to a single received narrative, in which it's hyper-violent and only happens to cis women—though in real life, it happens in a million different ways, and to all sorts of people.

But this isn't just about me narrowly avoiding a shitty trope. Bianca became more interesting to me, and her arc was clearer, when she was allowed to make mistakes without being pushed into them by outside forces.

Even when external forces do ruin a character's life—like a natural disaster, or a war, for example—we need to see them coming from a long way off. The characters themselves might ignore the signs of a growing crisis, but we still need to be aware of them before the nightmare arrives.

In general, before I unleash hell on a character, I ask myself: What am I hoping to get out of this? How is this going to advance the story, or this character's arc? Is this really the best way to get to where I'm trying to go?

When something good happens to a character, we all demand a high level of plausibility. Happy events must be "earned." Meanwhile, we require much less explanation when the world goes pear-shaped. Because when bad things happen, that's "realism."

If we don't feel it, it didn't happen

Remember how I said that suspension of disbelief is just as important for the writer as for the reader? That goes double when you're writing about unimaginable ordeals.

When something happens, we need to *feel* it as well as *see* it, and we need to believe in the consequences. In particular, we need to see how it affects the characters—since the whole point is to move the characters and their story forward, right?

I hate when a character goes through something unspeakable, and seems totally fine afterward. This reduces my ability to believe in both the character and the event. (And sure, sometimes people repress their trauma, but there are ways to show that's what's happening.) If a character just shakes off an ordeal like a wet dog, that's often a pretty good sign that the atrocities weren't necessary in the first place for the story. But sometimes, it can mean that a great story is going untold.

In real life, when you suffer the unendurable, you need to find a way to integrate it into your overall story, as painful as that sounds. You have to do the work of constructing what was happening before, and how the event unfolded, and put the incident into some kind of context. And then you have to do the work of understanding that you're safe now, which is an ongoing process.

Different people deal with trauma in different ways, and it's important not to present a one-size-fits-all healing process. In *The City in the Middle of the Night,* I was pretty careful to show Sophie, Mouth, and other characters having very different responses to the things they had gone through. I read *Trauma and Recovery* by Judith L. Herman, and a psychologist friend also recommended *The Body Keeps the Score* by Bessel van der Kolk, which I found an invaluable resource for understanding how we carry trauma in our bodies as well as our minds. I tried to pay attention to the small physiological cues that show that someone is re-feeling a terrible event.

Traumatized people tend to be more hyper-vigilant, and sometimes engage in more risk-taking behavior. (I learned a lot about this from talking to Sarah Gailey, while working on *City*.) A character could feel depressed and unable to concentrate, or could throw themself into work and push everything else to the side. How the character reacts to shitty experiences says something about who they are, and who they're going to become.

It's even more important to be mindful about trauma during a moment where the real world turns vicious, and cruelty becomes public policy. At such times, we need more than ever to understand the systems that turn people into predators, and the institutions that enable brutality. Don't just show us the worst things that can happen to people, show us the reasons *why* they happen. We need fiction that interrogates the layers of privilege and dehumanization that make some people seem to others like fair game for abuse.

But again, self-care is good writing practice. And you're under no obligation to make yourself sick writing about horrors while you're living through an actual horror movie.

At some point, we all started to think of violence and misery as the point of storytelling, rather than as a means to an end. Many writers (myself very much included) gloated endlessly about how much we love to "torture" our characters. We all talked about *Game of Thrones* as if the Red Wedding was what made it great—rather than our love for the characters. Comics creators spent decades steering superheroes toward a "grim 'n' gritty" aesthetic, while fantasy had to be "grimdark." The failure mode of prestige TV has sometimes been gratuitous darkness. And so on.

We started to treat ugliness as a key signifier of quality, rather than just one valid creative choice among many.

I increasingly find it helpful to think in terms of "options become constrained," rather than "things get worse." It's not so much that the situation deteriorates—it's more like doors are slamming shut, and the protagonists have fewer and fewer courses of action open to them. The rising sense of desperation is the most important thing, and there are a million ways to get there that don't risk making you more upset when the world is already upsetting enough.

■

CHAPTER 11

The Ending Is the Beginning

Life is full of mazes. You've probably had dozens of experiences that were bewildering and upsetting and glorious and dazzling at the time, and you just had to keep moving forward the best you could. And then you got to the end, and things made sense. You learned more information—but also, you knew how things turned out.

Once you've finished living through something, you can see the whole shape of it. You can turn it into a story.

The same is true of the stories that you make up out of whole cloth (or scraps of reality, as the case may be). You might have some idea of what the story is about—and in a later chapter, we're going to talk about intentionality—but when you get to the end, you can see all the pieces, including the ones that might not fit at all.

There's a good reason why one of the most common pieces of writing advice is to write the first draft as fast as possible, and then go back and revise: you don't even know what your story *is* until you know how it ends. Even if you outlined every last detail in advance, you won't know how an ending is going to work until you've actually written it.

How do you know when you've found a good ending? There are all kinds of criteria: a proper ending ought to wrap up some of the conflicts, or at least show how our understanding of them has changed. Big questions might need to be answered. The final page should probably leave us with a sense that the immediate crisis (whether of faith, love, identity, politics, or war) is over—or has reached a new phase.

But for my money, the best ending is the one that serves your characters best. They've been on a journey, and they've arrived, and they'll never be the same again. And they do something, or experience something, that lets us know how their voyage has transformed them, and maybe moved them closer to figuring themselves out. We haven't just been following a bunch of plot devices around, we've been following people—and we care about those people, and want to know how things turn out for them. The ending is the "how things turn out" part.

If I can know with some certainty where the characters started from, and where they land at the end of the story, then I can sketch out how they get from here to there. Especially if I've been sketching in some big character moments along the way that I can retroactively decide are part of this nice progression.

In the end, you want your cake to feel as if you used all the eggs, butter, sugar and flour that you showed the reader earlier. (Mmmmmm, cake.) That said, often it's better if some of the ingredients were only glimpsed in passing, or if the reader thought this was going to be a sponge cake and it ended up as a Bundt cake instead.

How I leveled up at writing endings

When I started out writing fiction, I decided to try and write one short story per week. I seldom hit that goal, but I did crank out a ton of short stories in a two-year period—and this meant I got a lot of invaluable practice at coming up with endings.

Looking back at all of those stories now, I can see how I slowly leveled up. And each of those levels represents a different aspect of bringing a story to a conclusion.

My first several endings involved my characters facing a dilemma at the start of the story, and then finding the solution at the very end.

In one of my earliest stories, a man is trying to understand why coffee loses all its flavor when it's zapped back to the time-traveling researchers who are living in the Paleolithic era. In the end, a random superspy (don't ask) accidentally shoots a cup of coffee, bathing it with negative ions, which turns out to be the key to protecting the coffee's flavor in the time vortex. Problem solved! There are some cute moments along the way—plus a wholesome appreciation of various different strains of coffee—but little or no character development.

At some point, I started getting more ambitious with my endings. Which meant, in practice, being more ambitious with my beginnings and middles. I started trying to layer in more emotional stakes and themes that the ending of the story could pay off. Often this was a bit crude—like, people would have an emotional epiphany that also allowed them to solve a plot problem. ("I realized that I'm not properly hearing my girlfriend express her emotional needs, and that lesson about active listening also helped me to realize I need to use a lower frequency to communicate with these mashed-potato aliens.")

And often, this also meant a lot of downer endings, as my characters confronted their own inability to change—this felt clever at the time, but now feels like a cop-out, because I was letting myself off the hook for my failure to write people who had enough of an inner life to allow for growth. (As bad as an unearned happy ending is, an unearned miserable ending is actually worse. I love a dark, ambiguous ending, but only if it's fully baked.)

One of those stories took place in a future where people only socialize online, and only with people who share their exact interests—but the main character has a torrid one-night stand with a man who turns out to be a "communitarian," or a believer in socializing with the people who happen to live in his local community. The two men form a real connection, but once the protagonist returns home, his distrust of communitarians gets the better of him, and he realizes he could never date someone who's not in his exact affinity group. So he ends up ghosting this lovely man, with whom he shared one perfect night.

For that sad ending to work, we'd have to invest in the relationship this guy throws away, and also feel him wrestling with the choice between love and ideology—and in retrospect, the story doesn't do any of that work.

At last, I leveled up again, and started being able to layer in more emotional and ideological struggles into the rest of the story, so the ending had more to work with. I've found that it's like a battery: the first nine-tenths of the story build up a charge as the characters keep thrashing against the constraints of their situation. The more energy the story has stored up, the flashier the bang I can get when I discharge it at the end.

I also learned, very much the hard way, that endings, even more than the rest of the story, required me to pay attention to my characters: What are they actually feeling, what do they really want, and what are they aware of at this point in the story? The closer I could get to answering those questions from my characters' perspectives—as opposed to my god's eye view as the author—the better the characters could surprise me at the end.

I don't think of a first draft as being finished until I have an ending that blows me away and makes me go, "YES THIS ONE YES." The right ending is often the fifth or sixth one that I come up with, and I have to keep going back, looking at everything I've been throwing into the story up to this point, and gaming out different scenarios. I often feel like the right ending is the one that requires a lot of attention to detail on my part, but also a willingness to take a wild leap into space.

You can change the question to fit the answer

So these days, I aim for the most intense, memorable, thought-provoking, ambitious ending I can cook up. And then my entire revision process is a matter of trying to make the rest of the story support that ending. If the ending relies on the reader being invested in the relationship between two characters, I'll go back and add more scenes of those characters getting to know each other. If a character needs to be an expert knife thrower at the end, then we damn well need to see her practicing knife throwing over the course of the story.

I decided while I was revising *All the Birds in the Sky* that the actual ending of the book takes place on pages 300–301 of the paperback edition: the moment when Laurence makes a choice that will shape the rest of his life, based on his feelings for Patricia. So a lot of my revisions were aimed at supporting that moment, by making sure their relationship was at the center of the

7 OTHER THINGS ABOUT ENDINGS THAT I'VE LEARNED THE HARD WAY

1. A good ending doesn't have to be a surprise, or a twist. The most gut-punchy finales are often the ones that you can kind of see coming, which only lends them more power when they arrive. If you do use a twist ending, the reader should still feel as if they should have seen it coming, because the clues were there all along.

2. You don't have to answer every last question, as long as the characters find some resolution. We don't care about the solution to every tiny mystery nearly as much as we do the emotional stakes that the characters have been chasing—and in real life, there are always a few things you'll never fully understand.

3. Likewise, you don't have to tie off every conflict with a bow, especially if the reader can easily see how things will

turn out. Sometimes leaving a little imaginative work for the reader to do can make them feel more invested, not less, in the story.

4. A denouement gives you a chance to wrap up more of the emotional questions in the story, after the main conflict has been put to bed. You can also drop some hints about how the characters will go on after the last page—and the denouement can pack more surprises, if the big plot resolution was more or less what people had expected.

5. An ending "pays off" if it addresses the things that you've told us, over the course of the story, that we should care about. If a character spent a hundred pages obsessing about learning the truth of her mother's death, we'll want to learn that truth by the last page.

6. Seven words sum up a really good landing: "Nothing will ever be the same again." A powerful work of art usually leaves you feeling like the characters, and maybe

book every step of the way. The actual plot, and the big questions of the book, are resolved several pages later, in a preposterous moment that I was absolutely terrified nobody would accept unless they'd already gotten an emotional catharsis from that earlier moment with Laurence. I sweated over both those resolutions, but I also tried to convince myself that if the first one felt satisfying enough, people would be willing to go with me for the second.

The good news: fiction writing is one of the few areas in life where you can change the question to fit the answer. You can't enter a random number at the bottom of your tax forms and then go back and change your yearly income and deductions to justify it (unless your accountant is an actual wizard). But you absolutely can arrive at an ending that tells the story you set out to tell, and then go back and rework everything that leads up to it so that it all holds together.

It's not about the end, it's about the center

I've stopped thinking of the process of writing a novel or short story as getting to the end—instead, I think of it as drilling down to the center.

As the story goes on and the characters (and I) learn more about what's at stake, we also burrow deeper into the unfinished business of the story, both emotional and thematic. And ideally, the center of the story is also the moment when the characters hit bottom. They've reached as much clarity as they ever could, they've gotten to the heart of their issues, and they're able to make choices that they couldn't have made before. At least, that's the hope.

When I think about my favorite endings in books, movies, TV—like the endings to *The Third Man, Blake's 7, The Good Place, The Four-Gated City, The Dispossessed,* and *Steven Universe*—the thing they have in common is that they feel right for the characters we've spent so much time with, and something happens that feels both stark and irrevocable. Someone dies, or something changes forever. The best endings don't compromise the integrity of the characters or the world, and also feel as if things couldn't have ended any other way.

And finally, a killer ending shows us what happens after the worst has happened. We might see something huge coming from a long way off—to the point where we start to dread it, or to be curious to know what'll happen when it arrives. A pretty good ending shows us what happens when that juggernaut in the distance shows up at last, but a *better* ending shows the fallout. All the consequences and reactions that we couldn't have

even the world, have gone through some changes, and there's no going back to the way things were before.

7. Your final sentences are like the last notes in a freaking symphony. (We're gonna keep coming back to music metaphors. Sorry not sorry.) If you can leave people with a final arresting image, but also with some lilt-tastic phrases that feel like the conductor is putting down their baton, you can leave the reader with a mood that'll stick around after the adventure is over.

expected. Especially when characters are forced to make some tough decisions, or to realize that they've been going about things the wrong way this whole time.

Unexpected but inevitable: that's the balance that most endings need to strike. Luckily, once you find that ending, you can always cheat and retroactively rework the rest of the story to plant all the clues and devices you'll need to make that magic trick succeed.

SECTION III

YOUR FEELINGS ARE VALID—AND POWERFUL

CHAPTER 12

⏳

Hold On to Your Anger. It's a Storytelling Gold Mine.

Years ago, I was struggling to find something to write. I'd run out of clever ideas—or maybe my particular brand of clever had stopped working for me. I was feeling stuck, confused, at a loss. I sat in front of a blank Word doc trying to brainstorm, and the most I could manage was a brain-squall. The harder I tried to make storytelling happen, the more frustrated I got, and the worse my struggle became.

Until I finally just asked myself: What am I mad about? And then the ideas just started pouring out of me.

If you listed your top ten favorite novels or stories, I pretty much guarantee at least a few of them were written because the author was pissed off about something, and just had to vent. Not only that, but I've found out the hard way that when I couldn't easily access any other emotion, I could always find my anger.

And that's bound to be the case when you're living through an ugly political moment, or a massive disaster. When everything is a rotten mess, you're bound to have a lot of steam to blow off. That's not always a nice feeling—but it's a damn storytelling gold mine.

In *Star Wars,* Yoda famously claimed that anger leads only to the dark side of the Force. But the Jedi Master was wrong: anger leads to everything good. Humor comes from anger (which is why so many comedians are deeply angry people). Great story conflicts come out of accessing your anger, too. And anger can be a way to access tenderness, kindness, protectiveness, and other "gentle" emotions. If you can get mad, you'll never run out of stories.

Neil Gaiman often tells the story of a giant clusterfuck that infuriated Terry Pratchett when he and Terry were touring to promote their novel *Good Omens*. When everything was finally resolved, Gaiman tried to suggest to Pratchett that he could stop being angry now, and Pratchett responded, "Do not underestimate this anger. This anger was the engine that powered *Good Omens*." Because humor comes from anger, and so does satire and an obnoxiously surreal sense of weirdness. Humor is a defense mechanism that allows us to lose our shit without losing our shit, and we've all been in situations where we can choose either to laugh or to scream.

To be clear: we're not just talking about losing your shit and vomiting your anger onto the page—though that can be freaking awesome and result in some powerful prose. We're also talking about filtering your so-called negative emotions through technique, and imagination, and using them as fuel to write all kinds of things—including plenty of scenes that your readers will come away from feeling calm, happy, and reassured.

You can absolutely be angry, and yet write a story that's not an angry story at all. I don't usually write about the thing I'm angry about, either—the thing about emotions is they're content-neutral. You can read the news, get super fired up about all the crimes and atrocities taking place in the world, and then channel all that emotional energy into writing a cute love story between a handsome elf and a frog-turned-prince.

I've written some of my sweetest, tenderest moments when I was just spitting with rage. That's due to the alchemy of emotions, whereby every emotion is connected.

Every other emotion is connected to anger somehow

Anger is like a primary color of emotion. If you can summon anger, you can write anything.

Take, for example, tenderness, or kindness. We're often at our angriest when we have something to protect or care for—and we all know that feeling when anger gives way to gentler emotions. Think of a mama bear shielding her young: you can feel the anger, but also glimpse the love, right under the surface. Not to mention, we get the angriest at the people whom we love the most.

Anger easily leads to remorse, too. And introspection and self-examination, as anyone who's ever gone off half-cocked and left a trail of destruction will testify. Master Yoda was right about one thing: anger has a direct link to fear, and every rage-out has a kernel of fear at its center.

The reverse is also true when it comes to joy—we've all experienced the moment when intense happiness turned to vitriol, because the rug got pulled out from under us. Even empathy can come from anger, because delving into the sources of your own rage can help you understand how others have been hurt and might lash out.

Once you've found your way from anger into one of these other emotions, you can skip the "anger" part on the page, unless it's actually part of the story. If you can find your way from anger to tenderness, then you can just write the tenderness into your narrative; you don't need to show your work.

For a lot of us, especially people who aren't cishet white men, anger is a huge taboo. We've been taught over and over that we should swallow our outrage. Marginalized people, in particular, are often told to censor our anger, or to act "reasonable" in the face of endless fuckery. When in fact the reverse is true:

it's on privileged people to be empathetic, to listen, and to pay attention to people who are coping with structural oppression.

I've never been great at expressing anger in real life, except for the occasional moment of snark, or stressed-out grouchiness. I was always kind of a pleaser, since childhood—even before I transitioned and started feeling all kinds of pressure to act more stereotypically female. But I've found that when I project my hottest, most choleric emotions onto the page, only good things happen.

Light some fires

I don't get all of my story ideas from asking myself what I'm angry about, or even most of them.

But when I am trying to capture a real intensity, that fire that makes stories come to life, it often comes down to reconnecting with my anger. A sense of urgency, desperation, or snarky humor can come out of touching that raw nerve. And when I'm trying to create a feeling of chaos and surprising twists and turns, it's not a bad thing to plug into that urge to flip some tables.

And it's the same when you're trying to create vivid scenes, with powerful details. The things that make you angriest are also likely to be some of your strongest, most powerful memories, because these things get burned into your brain. You can vividly remember what you were holding, what you were wearing, what you smelled, what you tasted, and everything that was going on in your head during a moment when something really pushed your buttons. And that's exactly the level of immediacy that you're aiming for in your storytelling. It's the intimacy of being right there in the middle of a bad situation.

In real life, upsetting and rage-inducing experiences are the most likely to get turned into capital-S Stories. That process whereby you spin raw sensory input and stream of consciousness moments into an anecdote that you can share with your astonished and outraged friends is the closest analog to what we all do when we try to turn a series of random events into an actual narrative.

And it probably goes without saying that your rage can help you write better villains, as well as figure out scenes where otherwise-sympathetic characters do something terrible or unforgivable in the heat of passion. If you want to get into the mindset of someone who's taking drastic action, it helps to have a direct line to some drastic feelings.

At the same time, though, your fury is also invaluable for writing about people standing up against oppression, or cruelty. It's natural to feel pissed off in the face of horrible abuses, like state-sponsored white supremacist violence and organized genocide—like the old bumper sticker says, "If you aren't outraged, you aren't paying attention."

There's a word for anger turned to constructive ends, and that word is "justice."

Channeling your anger can also be a way to cope with trauma, that doesn't have to involve re-traumatizing yourself. During those times when I've been really messed up by things that have happened to me—or by the state of the world—I've found that I've had more rage than I knew what to do with. So I channeled that rage into writing about people rising up, fighting back, doing the right thing, and this reminded me that I have more power than I realize. That together, we can tear down monuments and take down wannabe strongmen.

And screw anybody who wants to police your anger.

Find what pisses your characters off

We've already talked about finding characters, and helping them to evolve. Like Pokémon. But usually, the key to making a character really leap off the page is to find out what pisses them off. A living, breathing character needs to have stuff that sticks in their metaphorical craw, like pet peeves, or baggage. And when outrageous things happen, they probably need to become outraged.

Often as not, when I have a character who's not clicking, it's because I haven't found what they're angry about yet.

My favorite fictional characters are the ones who cannot witness evil being done without becoming fired up about it, and I have all the time in the world for characters who will go to the ends of the Earth to right a wrong. But I also have boundless love for characters who hold petty grudges, who are still stewing about something that happened to them in seventh grade, or who are just grumpy cusses. A character who is supposed to save the world, but can't let go of an incredibly minor vendetta, is automatically fascinating. And utterly believable. That's the great thing about anger, after all: it doesn't really come with a sense of proportion.

As a general rule of thumb, the "nicer" the character, the harder I have to work to find that little nugget of animosity inside them. I've found this is especially important for characters who would never dream of actually hulking out. The angriest people are sometimes the ones who never raise their voices at all.

When it comes to some marginalized characters, though, I've run into the opposite problem. In one of my unpublished novels, a generous friend pointed out to me that one of my supporting characters was a stereotypical "angry Black woman," rather than the rich and layered character I'd convinced myself I was writing.

This book is all about surviving rough times by losing yourself in story-craft. And it's all too easy to think that means channeling only sweetness and light, or tuning out all the negativity in the world in favor of escapist fun. Which is awesome, if that's what you want to do. But if you're spitting mad about all the truly disgusting things happening around you, then I have some good news for you: that anger might just help you to write something truly righteous, in every sense of the word.

CHAPTER 13

People Are Only as Interesting as Their Relationships

I don't write characters. I write relationships.

When I realized this, a great many things fell into place for me, and I started to find my groove as a fiction writer. These days, whenever I start a new story, I try to figure out the main relationship, or set of relationships, that the narrative will revolve around, like a center of gravity. It's easy enough to track one character's arc, and show how someone changes from the first sentence of the story to the last—but I have way more fun tracking the twists and turns of their relationship with another person.

Part of this is because I love writing a good conversation, or any scene involving two or three people having emotionally charged interactions. And I live for those moments where the dynamic between two people shifts, or they recognize that they've arrived at a new place together. You can only write so many scenes where someone changes how they relate to the concept of Duty, or Honor, or to their job—abstract concepts and plot devices don't talk back, and don't have their own perspective.

We've all been force-fed the myth of the Loner, or the Rugged Individual, and I have a soft spot for stories about one person lost in the ruins, à la the first half of *I Am Legend*. As I discussed in chapter three, I was that nerdy queer kid with a learning disability who always wandered lonely as a cloud—so I definitely feel an affinity for that loner archetype.

Still, I've found out the hard way that we're nothing without family, friendships, love. And during those times when our entire nation is turning into one big human centipede, we need each other more than ever. Our loved ones and boon companions should be there to support us and remind us of who we are, in the face of all the lies the world tries to force-feed us.

We need enough books about the power of human connection to build a tower that reaches all the way to the thermosphere. There can never be enough stories about characters building rapport, and learning to see outside themselves, and finding their people, and saving each other. I want to feel the complexities and challenges—and, yeah, the horrible aspects, too—of human contact. Most of us feel isolated and set apart from each other, even when there's no social distancing, so I crave storytelling that speaks to the ways that we are all connected—even if, inevitably, fictional characters will misunderstand and betray everyone in their lives.

A good summary of a lot of my favorite stories is: "Two or more people learn to see each other more clearly." Relationships are what I show up for, as a writer and as a reader. Anybody who's ever read, or written, fanfiction will know that romances and intense friendships (and frenemy-ships) are what we're all here for.

Years ago, I read an interview where someone asked Iris Murdoch why she wrote so many stories about romantic relationships. There was a definite note of condescension in the way the interviewer asked this question, as if Murdoch was wasting her talents writing glorified romance novels—or maybe, as if a lady novelist couldn't hope to tackle weightier topics, such as war. Or business. Murdoch responded that love is all there is, that it's the most important thing in the world, and the biggest subject one could write about. This made a huge impression on me, and the longer I carry on in the writing racket, the more I feel like it's true: there's no topic as significant as love—though I'd include friendship and fellowship as types of love that are worth rejoicing over.

Or if you want a more science-fictional reference, the original *Star Trek* didn't become a great TV show until writer Gene L. Coon started deepening the camaraderie between Kirk, Spock, and McCoy.

How to find a great love (or friendship) story

I try to pick the smallest possible number of relationships to weave a story around, and then I keep nurturing them until they take on a life of their own. Relationships are like any other element: the more of them you have in a story, the harder it is to give each one the space it deserves.

When it comes to short stories, I often pick one pair whose ties will inform the entire narrative. But in a novel, there tend to be more relationships to track, especially if there's more than one protagonist. A single character might have workplace relationships as well as extracurricular ones, and you have to pay at least some attention to all of them.

How do you figure out which relationship to focus on? And once you've found the pairing(s) you want to highlight, how do you strengthen their dynamic and troubleshoot any problems? The answer to both questions is the same. You do for fictional relationships the same thing you do for real ones: 1) look for chemistry, 2) spend lots of time together, and 3) try and infuse every interaction with meaning.

Chemistry is obviously a "know it when you see it" thing—Tinder and OkCupid wouldn't be raking in nearly as much cash if it were easy to find romantic chemistry in real life. Still, I get curious about a relationship for the same reasons I get curious about an individual character: if there is a detail, or some piece of unfinished business, or a question in my head about a particular pairing, then I want to see more of those two people interacting.

Also, the best relationship to focus on is usually the one that brings out something unexpected in one or both characters. If you find yourself writing a moment where you see a side to a character you've never seen before, or you say to yourself, "Wow, I didn't know they felt that way," then that's a good sign that these two fictional creations need to spend a lot more time together.

What if two characters ought to have a lot to say to each other in theory, but in practice their scenes are dull? Could be there's just no chemistry, and your protagonist needs to get out there and start seeing other people. Or maybe there's something wrong with one or both characters: like, maybe one character is too much of a doormat, or lets everybody else get away with too much. One or both of those characters might be more one-dimensional than you let yourself believe.

It's always worth asking, How does this relationship help both of these characters? What do they get from each other that they can't get elsewhere? Do they have a choice about being together—and if they do, why do they keep hanging out?

And as for "**spending more time together**" . . . I'm a big fan of sticking two characters in the same place, and watching what happens. But sometimes, I need to put some thought into crafting moments, or reasons, for them to be together. Giving a duo a problem that they have to team up to solve can lead to some fun back-and-forth, and so can creating a situation where they want opposite things and have to work it out. One of the best uses for plot devices is just giving characters unfinished business, or something that they want from each other.

There's nothing wrong with trapping two people down a well and forcing them to talk things out. (In fiction, I mean. Don't go doing that in the real world, because the neighborhood association might object.)

Still, a particular duo might only get to have two or three scenes together in an entire novel, for plot or logistical reasons. It's up to you to make sure each of those scenes feels like a Turning Point in their relationship, rather than a moment where they're treading water. Make each exchange count, so that sparks always seem to fly when they're together, and the reader will come away from the book feeling as if their dynamic was important to the story.

My favorite pairings, hands down, are the ones where every interaction advances the themes or ideas of the story, or speaks to something the characters are struggling with. Think Mulder and Scully in *The X-Files*, Jane and Katherine in *Dread Nation*, or Catra and She-Ra in *She-Ra and the Princesses of Power*.

The spikiest interactions often come from characters who are on the opposite sides of an argument (especially if both sides might have some merit). Any time I can give people a philosophical disagreement, or two contrasting worldviews, I get excited to watch them hash it out. Especially if their interactions are emotionally charged, and they actually like each other.

And those last two pieces are important. Nobody wants to read hundreds of pages of a Socratic dialogue between two characters who represent Progress Versus Tradition or whatever. (Okay, I might read that book. But I'm in the minority, I'm guessing.) The scenes where people hash out their disagreements should be as much about feelings as anything else, and we need to feel the characters' investment in each other.

Plus in real life, people seldom hold Debates using parliamentary rules. People talk around and beside what's really bugging them, and maybe only let slip their real issues in the middle of ranting about five other things. And meanwhile, I find it exhausting to spend time with people who just don't enjoy each other at all. Even if two characters ostensibly hate each other's guts, and even if you've trapped them down a well, we need to glimpse the "fr-" part of "frenemy," or it's just going to be a giant bummer.

Conflict and affection: the magnetic forces that push characters apart and then drag them together again.

Strong people dote on their friends and loved ones

Writers often overemphasize the "conflict" part of storytelling over the "caring" part. I already ranted about the surplus of "grimdark" storytelling in recent years, but in addition to all the maiming and sexual assault, we've also sat through endless petty thunderdomes, full of people tearing each other down.

There's a reason why Becky Chambers' space-opera novels felt like such a breath of fresh air: she shows people caring about and nurturing their crewmates. I've lost count of how many times I've heard people say in recent years that they crave "chosen family" and kindness in storytelling, which is why I've been living for shows like *The Baby-Sitters Club* and *Julie and the Phantoms*.

When the world turns into a cheap mockbuster version of an apocalyptic dystopia, we all want to be strong. We want to be survivors. But you know what strong people do? They take care of their friends and loved ones, and they look out for people who need extra help and support.

Human connection. It's the whole fucking ball game.

I've taken special care in my fiction to show that men can be caring, especially cishet white men. Men can be nurturing. Men can be self-effacing and kind and vulnerable. My favorite romance novel of the past few years is *An Extraordinary Union* by Alyssa Cole, in large part because Malcolm is never a flaming superdick, even in the interests of ramping up the intensity of the conflict. As long as our books (and movies and TV shows) only show men being tiresome bastards, real-life dudes will continue to take away the message that shitty behavior is part of being a man. And let's kick the "smartest man in the room" out of the room.

On a similar note, I am here for more positive depictions of sexuality that foreground consent and mutual respect. When people hook up, I like to see them negotiate and learn more about each other, and also use safer-sex supplies. And even when people aren't actually hooking up, if they're just flirting or dancing or joking around, their sexual tension doesn't have to be creepy, and nobody needs to act like a predator. The same way that I care about characters who care about each other, I am ride-or-die for protagonists who aren't creeps (unless being a creep is the point of their character). There are lots and lots of ways to bring intensity and sparks to an interaction—see above, re: characters not agreeing on everything—without anyone needing to groom anyone else, or act like a slimeball.

Relationships are also a chance to feature LGBTQIA+ peeps, and to show queer romances that don't end in tragedy for tragedy's sake. They're an opportunity to celebrate different body types, including fat and disabled bodies.

And finally, friendships can be romantic. Friendships can be as intense and beautiful as any love affair. (One of my unpublished novels is about three people who are in a "platonic love triangle" where they love each other, without any sexual or romantic component.) I am here for friends who break up, misunderstand each other, betray each other, realize they can't live without each other, tearfully reunite and team up to save each other, and then do the whole thing all over again. When we talk about relationships, it's easy to default to thinking about partners and sexual/romantic liaisons, but friendship is *life*.

A great relationship has twists and turns, heart and substance, blood and spit and tears. Anyone can write a plot twist, but showing how a relationship changes and grows is the most beautiful thing a story can do, and the best medicine during a sickening historical moment.

CHAPTER 14

■

One Easy Way to Feel Better About the World

The world can be a scary place sometimes. There are carnivorous office pigs with razor-sharp key-fob teeth, and fifty-foot-tall swans keep scooping people up in their palatial bills. Dirt bikes have come to life, ridden by people made of dirt, and they want to turn everything into dirt. But there is one easy, and hopefully fun, way to feel less despondent—and to get in touch with your own sense of optimism and possibility.

You can write about people who want things.

This is one of the main reasons why fiction is great: it allows us to model desire. People in stories generally have goals—even if they struggle, even if they face setback after setback. They have dreams and wishes and hopes. They strive toward something that they've enshrined in their hearts.

A lot of writing advice talks about motivations. We talk endlessly about finding your character's motivation, and making sure your characters have motivations that are clear to the reader. Or if the characters are ambivalent or torn, as is frequently the case, we understand what they're torn between, or what they're ambivalent about.

But instead of talking about motivation, let's talk about desire. Ambition. Lust. Craving. Yearning. We can stop being so technical or polite, and start talking about raw, naked, shameless *want*.

It's no accident that many of my favorite characters have their hearts set on a prize, and let nothing stand in their way. Lately, I'm taking a lot of solace in reading young adult novels in which the main characters chase their dreams with a recklessness.

Your characters' desires don't have to be reasonable or fair—in fact, it's often better if their goal is something we know they can't, or shouldn't, attain. I obsess way too often about Wreck-It Ralph's quest for a ribbon that says "HERO," which is obviously not going to fix his life, but which represents a longing that I can feel in my bones. Even if someone's goal is actually terrible, we can sympathize with them, or at least understand their point of view. And we can get wrapped up in their struggle to achieve their goal, even if the judgy part of our brains disapproves.

Desire is an important part of story writing, and it's a major part of the emotional landscape of any story that's not unbearably bleak and drab. Writing about fictional desire can be a source of comfort and a good reminder that it's okay to have dreams and desires of your own.

When the world turns into an actual trash fondue, I find myself getting scared to wish for anything. As if I could be tempting fate if I harbored any ambitions. Or maybe it just feels selfish to want more, when so many people are suffering. Plus, people from marginalized groups have been told over and over that our desires are not valid and our dreams are unreasonable—that's part of the stigma of marginalization.

So those moments when I most feel trapped at the rock bottom of Maslow's hierarchy of goddamn needs? Those are the exact moments when I find it healing and freeing to imagine a character who goes for what they want, shamelessly and ruthlessly.

You can't get what you want if you don't know what you want

I've been working on another fantasy novel for grown-ups lately, and I'm excited to explore the notion that doing magic requires you to focus your intent. You only have power if you can figure out what you want, and can express your wishes clearly. This, in turn, requires people to admit what they actually want, and to believe that they deserve to have it. I've found this an especially comforting metaphor, while I've been hiding from the dirt people riding their dirt bikes to dirt town.

Perhaps the most frustrating, and yet also the most thrilling and therapeutic, aspect of fiction writing is drilling down to the core of your characters' cravings. This is one of the trickiest aspects of troubleshooting, in general—a story where the characters have flat or muddled desires is liable to be dull, even if the plot and world-building are both resplendent.

(Again, I've got nothing against ambivalent characters—but ambivalence is not the same thing as having no goals whatsoever. A character could be struggling to make sense of a confusing stew of impulses and passions, or they could have repressed their feelings to the point where they can't admit what they want. Either of those things is interesting in a way that "I want to stumble glassy-eyed from plot point to plot point" isn't.)

So how do you figure out what your characters want? By figuring out who they *are*. Their desires come out of their backstory, their ideologies, their identities, or their self-images.

Something happened to them when they were younger, and they desperately want to make it right.

Or they're invested in seeing themselves as the champions of the downtrodden, to the point where they will go to the ends of the Earth to right a wrong.

Or perhaps they're in love, or they crave power, or they need revenge, or they want to get back a stolen family heirloom.

You know that action-movie cliché where the hero shakes their fist at the camera and says, "This time . . . it's personal"? In a good story, it's personal *every time*. It's much easier to stan characters who have a deep emotional connection to whatever they're chasing. They're not just on a quest because they got some "call to adventure" nonsense, but because they feel positively itchy with need for something that will complete them.

As with most other aspects of writing, I have a tendency to get this wrong, at least at first. I'll assign goals to my characters that don't actually hold up over the course of a story. I'm brilliant at trying to force my protagonists to want what I think they should want, rather than what they actually do want. Often, my characters are more selfish than I think they ought to be, and I have to stop being so judgmental.

But sometimes it goes the other way: in early drafts of my young adult novel *Victories Greater Than Death,* I realized that some of my teens from Earth were being too petty and self-centered when they were encountering injustice and misery on a galactic scale. When I allowed them to be more outraged, and to thirst for justice more openly, they started coming to life in a whole new way.

Still, a character's aspirations can be more personal, and more self-centered, than the overall stakes of the story. Take the original *Star Wars*: neither Luke Skywalker nor Han Solo is motivated by a desire to blow up the Death Star. Luke wants to escape the moisture farm and follow in his father's footsteps, while Han wants to get paid so Jabba doesn't turn him into an ornament. Their goals end up aligning with the Death Star demolition, especially Luke's—but Han is arguably a more interesting character, because he wants something beyond the confines of the movie's plot.

I often get a lot of juice out of the tension between what particular characters are after on the one hand, and the thing the story needs them to chase on the other. The disconnect between stakes and motivations can be a source of energy: we've all yelled at the screen or the page, while characters dwelled on their own personal issues while we knew that an army of goblins was about to smash their hometown. You can get a lot of good suspense out of waiting for the characters' goals and the larger stakes of the story to align. And it's easier to identify with characters whose concerns are smaller and more individual than whatever grand thing the story is trying to get them to chase.

Desire is complicated and messy, and that's why it's so great

All storytelling comes down to conflict, one way or another. You and I both want to be Homecoming Queen, but only one of us can wear the crown. I very much do not want to be Homecoming Queen, but winning the crown is the only way to save the school from falling into a radioactive chasm. I want to be Homecoming Queen, but my death-cult-priestess mother believes that such celebrations are vain and idolatrous, and has forbidden me from participating.

There are always going to be other people who don't want us to achieve our goals. Desire is constantly at war with fear and guilt in most people. And life is full of situations where we have to choose between two mutually exclusive goals—like going to college, versus going on tour with your neo-skiffle band.

Like Faulkner said, good storytelling is all about aortic civil wars.

I'm all in for characters who feel guilty for their desires. I'm also a fan of characters who know that their passions are selfish and wrong, but they just don't freaking care. And characters who chase something they've been taught is immoral have my axe every time—like Yetu, the hero of Rivers Solomon's excellent *The Deep,* who defies tradition and flees from her appointed role as the keeper of her people's worst memories.

Years of storytelling have conditioned us to expect heroes to

FOUR QUESTIONS TO KEEP ASKING

Your characters shouldn't just have hopes and wishes—they should also have strong feelings about their situation. So here are four questions I keep asking about my characters:

1. How do they feel about their situation?
2. What do they do about that feeling?
3. What result does their action have?
4. How do they feel about this new situation?

I try to play as many rounds of this game as I can, with a character, to get in an action-oriented mindset. When I have a story that feels dead on the page, I've found this diagnostic surprisingly effective—because often the problem is that I haven't nailed down how a character really feels about their situation, and what that feeling might spur them to do.

Your characters' attempts to change their circumstances suffer or cause misery when they run toward their goals—especially if they've defied convention, their friends' wishes, or their own hang-ups in the process. And this can be a great source of character growth (again, see *Wreck-It Ralph,* which really is a masterclass in motivation and transformation).

But especially during a trash-fondue era, when everyone is being punished for just existing, there's something wonderful about watching a character level up, or achieve at least a partial victory. Especially if this character is the sort of person who'll get called a "Mary Sue" by online misogynists for the crime of attaining any amount of power or satisfaction. A partial victory can be as satisfying as a complete one, especially in the middle of a story.

I also like a good ratio of setbacks to power-ups. The principle of variable reward teaches us that we're more likely to get addicted to pushing a lever if we get a peanut only every other time, or every few times. If every time we push the lever, we might get a peanut, an electric shock, or nothing, we'll keep pushing that lever until it breaks. The same is true for getting yourself hooked, as a reader or writer, on a character's struggles.

Once your characters are fired up with the need to achieve something or prevent something, that will help you, the storyteller, to know what it is that *you* care about. What are *you* might fail, or backfire—and it's often more interesting if that's the case—but we still need to understand their viewpoint, and witness the actions it spurs them to.

hoping will happen, and what does the narrator think about all this? (Yes, you and the narrator are frequently two different people.) The best stories are a giant stew of unrealistic and unreasonable wishes on the part of the characters, the narrator, the author, the readers, and the universe. It's fun to watch them all collide and hopefully explode—and getting in touch with fictional desire might just help you to feel like you can want things in real life, too.

CHAPTER 15

Revision Is the Process of Turning Fake Emotion into Real Emotion

Every Pixar movie I've ever seen has made me cry like a molly-soaked debutante. I managed to score a limited-edition T-shirt of Bing Bong from *Inside Out*—but I've hardly ever worn it, because the sight of that cheery face makes me shed enough tears to fill a jumbo popcorn bucket. When I talk to folks who work at Pixar, I always hear all about how every single moment of their films gets poked and prodded and questioned and re-worked, to make sure it holds up. Because even the most apparently simple moment of heartbreak or squee requires a ton of second-guessing and careful thought.

I feel like I never really get the emotions right on the first—or even second—pass of a story. My first drafts are usually just a bunch of events, in the rough order that I think they happen in. I have to go back and keep digging deeper, and paying closer attention, to make the feels come through. It's just way too easy for me to fool myself into thinking that I've written a vivid emotional moment, when in fact I've written a weaksauce early-'90s-video-game cut scene.

For me, the revision process is all about turning the fake emotion of the first draft into something real. Something that other people can (hopefully) get sucked into. This is one reason I share my work with a small army of beta readers and sensitivity readers and the bison in Golden Gate Park, before I inflict it on my editors: to catch any fakery early. (Those bison are a super insightful audience, I read to them as often as I can.)

Why is it so hard to get real emotion on the page? There's this layer of distance between you and the thing you're writing that can only be bridged by a lot of concentration and self-awareness and daydreaming and zoning out and trying to get into character. (Because like I said, writing is acting.) You always have the ideal version of any story in your head, and it's vivid and operatic and huge and colorful. And then you try to write it down, and it's . . . a jumble of things happening and people talking, and where did that lush musical score go, anyway?

Gut checking your big emotional moments can be an essential part of getting lost in your own story. Which is important, if you're writing stories as a way of holding yourself together in the eye of a landfill tornado.

As with everything else to do with writing, there could be any number of reasons why the emotions aren't showing up. But there are a few major ways to catch undercooked moments: 1) Spending more time on the events leading up to them. 2) Concentrating on the little details. 3) Understanding what really pushes your characters' buttons.

It's all about the lead-up

As I mentioned before, I sometimes outline stories and novels before I start writing—but I will always make a very detailed outline after I've already written a complete draft. And sometimes again, after the second draft.

I do this for a bunch of reasons. I want to make sure all of the big plot points hold water. (One fun trick: try outlining the whole thing backward, from the end to the beginning, and stick the word "because" in between each big event. "This happens, because this happens, because . . .") I'll also outline from the point of view of the antagonist, or a supporting character, to see if these events make sense from their point of view. And as I'll discuss in a later chapter, I also make sure each section of the story is the approximate right length.

But the main reason for outlining after I write is to figure out what the big emotional "beats" are. And then to make sure that the rest of the story actually supports them. I can look at those beats holistically and see them in the context of the rest of the story.

Even when I've outlined meticulously before I started writing, I might not know for sure what the most heart-exploding moments are on the first go-round. Nor do I know the exact order things need to happen in, because little things always shift around. All too often, that little scene that I thought was just filler turns out to be the last time that two characters get a chance to talk to each other before something huge and terrible (or awesome) happens. Even more frequently, I realize there's a scene missing, and two people need to talk before they're thrown into the deep end.

Meanwhile, I can't always get the emotions down pat until I know how the characters are gonna end up—because part of the purpose of these heartfelt moments is to justify and set up the decisions they're going to make. If I know that one person stabs (or kisses) another, then I need to give them some juicy interactions before that happens.

Another way of looking at it: these emotional beats are the heart of the story, and everything else is the vascular system that makes them work. Or if your story is a piece of music, the most heartfelt or intense moments are the melodic hook, and all the other moments are the bass line, the drums, the keyboard and horn fills. And possibly the strings, if you're going old school. Every part of the story helps to build a mood—and that mood, in turn, helps make the smooching or processing or fighting feel earned.

It's really about tracking the relationships between these characters, so you can find the turning points, and the defining moments between them.

Big emotions come from tiny things

The bigger the emotion you're trying to evoke, the more attention you need to pay to the smallest things. This is true in two different ways: each moment needs to be grounded in real sensory details, and there need to be small clues and barely noticeable moments leading up to a huge emotional climax.

The texture of reality is made out of random details, and it's especially weird what you'll notice when your emotions are working overtime. You might be in the middle of a relationship-ending fight with your partner, but your eye might land on a tiny candy wrapper on the sidewalk, being scooted forward by the wind. Or you might be intensely aware of the smell of sweat and craft beer from a nearby nightclub. Or you might find yourself remembering a broken shoelace from a pair of shoes you owned a dozen years ago.

Incidentally, smells are *awesome*. Nothing anchors you to a particular moment in time like a really powerful scent. Whenever I smell a certain brand of vanilla-hazelnut coffee, I'm instantly transported back in time to the church choir I sang in as a kid, with a vividness that no visual stimulus could ever evoke. Music and certain sounds can also plug you into a memory: there's one Earth, Wind & Fire song that I can never listen to without thinking of someone I broke up with many years ago.

People are really prone to projecting huge emotions onto random tiny objects. Maybe it's because you can't wrap your mind around the vastness of what you're feeling, but one way or another, little touchstones and cultural references gain emotional significance over time. These items might be connected to a particular person, or they could just evoke a particular sentiment.

We tend to deflect their emotions in other ways, too. Someone might be really pissed that their bae ditched them at a nightclub to go snort coke in a graveyard, but might only complain about the way their bae slurps their soup. Or they might not be able to express the scope of their gratitude or love for another person, so they might just lavish way too much praise on that person's shoes. You can use the awkwardness of expressing real-life emotion to offset a lot of the awkwardness of capturing emotion in fiction.

There's also the common trick of showing someone's emotions by describing the thing they're looking at through their eyes. A character can stare at the exact same wall, and the bricks might look dirty and crumbling or bright red and homey, depending on the beholder's emotional state.

You can also use tiny, barely noticeable moments to keep emotions simmering before they finally reach a full boil. They don't even have to feel like a slow ratcheting up of tension. As I've said before, I enjoy putting two characters together and just deepening the content, and the subtext, of their interactions, until I (and hopefully any eventual readers) want to see what's going to happen with them. A random scene of two people debating grapefruits versus tangerines can deepen my investment in their dynamic, if their personalities are on display.

And finally, if there's an object that's important to your story, it needs to be important to your characters—and ideally not just as a means to an end. We'll care about the crystal goblet of the Troll Overlord if your characters care about it, not just because we love crystal goblets. Especially if the goblet has a personal significance that goes beyond its usefulness in the plot, like it's part of a dinnerware set that used to belong to someone's family.

Don't be afraid to push your characters' buttons

When I'm revising, I'll often do a "feels" pass, in which I go through scene by scene, and think about the emotion that I'm trying to convey. How do my characters feel at this point in the story? What's actually going through their heads, and how is the emotion hitting them?

The most potent reactions are both psychological and physiological. Which is another way of saying that a really strong emotion hits you in both your head and your guts.

I dearly love characters who overthink things, and I'm always here for a ranting inner monologue. As a neurotic overthinker and secret introvert, I naturally identify with people who are in their own head a lot. And I love wry ironic asides, too. So when someone is feeling something, I don't just want to get a sense of inchoate emotion—I bond with characters who are thinking

GETTING INTO CHARACTER

When an actor needs to bring a lot of emotion to a scene, they'll submerge themself in their character, trying to live in their skin and access all the pent-up emotion they're bringing to a moment. But they'll also reach for their own personal experiences and emotions.

When *Supernatural* was coming to an end at long last, Jared Padalecki gave an interview to TVLine where he talked about a season-two episode, "Heart," in which Sam Winchester needed to cry on screen. Padalecki told TVLine that he thought about "what it would be like to put my dog down," and "what it would be like to love something, or to care about something deeply, and have to say goodbye to it."

Padalecki's performance in that scene is heartrending, and even elicited an unplanned tear from Jensen Ackles. So when you're trying to bring a lot of emotion to a scene, borrow a trick from Sam Winchester and imagine (or remember) something intense in your own life. through what they're feeling in the moment, or immediately afterward.

Like if a first-person narrator says, "I thought falling in love would be like drinking ten milkshakes, but it's actually more like drinking a gallon of expired cough syrup. I'm light-headed and nauseous and my insides are all pink."

There's an unspoken taboo against characters just coming out and saying what they're feeling—because it's often too flat, or matter-of-fact, to say, "I was really angry." That does sound like a robot describing human emotions. But when a character has had a strong internal monologue, or a lot of self-awareness, then hearing their inner voice saying, "This sucks," or "This isn't fair," or "I didn't think I could ever be this happy," packs a surprising amount of power. We're privy to what they're telling themself about this feeling they're having.

As for the physiological . . . I already mentioned feeling nauseous and light-headed. Strong emotions live in your body as much as your mind. When I've been really pissed, I've actually felt overheated and like my head was full of noise. When I get ashamed, my face really does feel hot.

When I was a kid, I found a book at a yard sale called *Ann Landers Talks to Teenagers About Sex*. And it contained an amazing letter a kid named Randy wrote to Ann Landers about his crush on a girl named Dottie. When Randy looks at Dottie, he gets weak in the knees and light-headed. He's lost all appetite, and sweats constantly. The punch line: "It wasn't love at all. It was the flu." I always think about Randy's fauxmance whenever I write about people feeling genuine romantic passions.

So when I go back and add more intensity to the emotions in a scene during revisions, I'll think about the psychological and physiological stuff. I'll also try to see past my own hang-ups.

I love my characters and want them to have a smooth ride, so I'll often make them nicer to each other, and calmer in the face of extreme shit, than they realistically should be. I also fail to think about what the characters know, what they believe, and what they're hoping and fearing at this point in the story.

[Minor spoilers for *The City in the Middle of the Night* follow . . .]

In *The City in the Middle of the Night,* Bianca thinks that Sophie is dead, until Sophie suddenly shows up to warn her that she's been betrayed. In the first few versions of that scene, Bianca understands the situation instantaneously: Sophie has faked her death and hidden herself from Bianca. But when I thought more about it, I realized that Bianca, based on the information she had, would assume that Sophie had been imprisoned this whole time.

As soon as I could see the situation from Bianca's perspective, her reaction was suddenly a lot more natural—and jumping to the wrong conclusion made the truth hit her harder.

I was on a writing panel a few years ago with Curtis Chen, author of the Kangaroo series, and he offered a great tip: if you really want to get better at writing strong emotions, read a ton of romance novels. Not only are romance novels some of the best reads out there, they're a masterclass in feels.

And don't be afraid to show people being sappy and shmoopy and even cutesy. Otherwise, your writing is just plain unrealistic—because in real life, when people are under pressure, they get gushy and demonstrative af. People who are in deep shit up to their armpits will pour their hearts out to each other, and they usually don't stop to think about whether some critic on the other side of the third wall is going to complain about too much sweetness.

Likewise, joy is an essential part of your emotional palette.

People who feel bitterness and misery but not joy are dull, and unpleasant to spend time with. The worst emotions hit harder if we've seen these characters experiencing delight. Don't forget: a roller coaster has to go up as well as down, or it's just a road with a sharp gradient.

CHAPTER 16

Twelve Ways to Keep the Fun of Writing Alive

Lately people keep asking me one question: how can we avoid writing burnout, when everything is one big trash-volcano? Okay, *two* questions. People also want to know the best way to make tiny pro-wrestler costumes for their thumbs—because thumb wrestling is getting seriously artisanal lately.

But that first question, about avoiding burnout, is a big deal. Especially when most forms of engagement with the world seem to turn into doomscrolling. When I keep saying, in these essays, that stories are a lifeline, and the worlds you create could help save your life (and maybe other people's), that might sound like a heavy responsibility that must be Taken Seriously. And we all know the road to burnout-ville is paved with pressure and excessive seriousness.

So here are a dozen tricks I've found to keep writing fun, and joyful—and most of all, irresponsible.

1) Change your reward structure

We tend to think of writing like jogging—how many miles did you cover? Did you get a cramp and just keep going through the pain? But writing isn't like that. It's more like doing a jigsaw puzzle where we have to carve the pieces as we assemble them, and some of the pieces will turn out to belong to a different puzzle entirely.

So I've changed how I think about productivity. A good writing session can consist of all kinds of things, including rethinking, brainstorming, editing, and even just staring into space. I used to obsess about my word count—the raw number of new words I had added to the project—until I realized that some of my best writing experiences were ones in which almost no new words of story were added, but I had a clearer sense in my head of what shape the story should take.

I stopped beating myself up for woolgathering when I ought to be putting words down—because I realized that falling into a kind of trance is often the best way to find new ideas. And sometimes deleting 1,000 words was more valuable than writing 1,000 new words. Sometimes I just needed to spend some quality time going back and rereading what I'd already written, to get the story fresh in my head again.

Especially during times when a flood of bad news makes it hard to produce piles of words, I've stopped thinking of myself as a machine that needs to crank out enough widgets. I still produce a lot of words—in fact, I've found that a day of rumination or reworking is often followed by a really prolific session, with just words piled on words. I had a lovely online conversation with *The Invisible Life of Addie LaRue* author V. E. Schwab, who showed off her chart of writing time—based on a goal of two hours' writing time at a go, rather than a particular word count.

Back in the chapter on imposter syndrome, we touched on people telling you that you're not a real writer—but it's worth repeating here that this is a silly notion. Some writers write every day, others a few times a month. It's all about what works for you.

And meanwhile, I've also thought more about the "rewards" part of my reward structure. I eat plenty of chocolate, but I also take dance breaks, or get up and take a little walk, or do something else physical. I have a friend who watches an episode of their favorite sitcom after ninety minutes of writing. I try to find rewards that are fun (so I associate writing with fun activities) and can help loosen me up, to avoid the dreaded stiff-neck syndrome.

2) Try some low-stakes, instant-gratification story writing

Long before I thought of myself as a writer, I was always making up stories. When I start to get sick of trying to Produce a Finished Product, I try to go back to just making up stories, without any goal or ambition in mind.

During non-pandemic times, I host a reading series where I invent fictional bios for all the writers, using a mixture of over-preparation and improv. But it's just as much fun to make up a story on the spot when I'm hanging out with friends. Sometimes we'll hang out and play a storytelling game, like *slash: romance without boundaries*. Or a tabletop role-playing game.

Making up stories is both easy and fundamentally silly, as we proved with our hundred story ideas about a potato. There was a fish that thought it was a rock. There was a woman who only sang in her sleep. If you have kids, make up stories to tell them at bedtime. Make those kids *earn* their unfeasibly sugary breakfast cereal. Do whatever you can to make story-invention a thing you just do, for fun as well as Serious Art.

Like Parliament says, "Fun will take the longer way around."

3) Cheat on your current project

Seriously. Cheat like a husband in a Dolly Parton song. If you're forcing yourself to keep pushing and prodding at your current manuscript in progress, and you're *not* up against an imminent deadline, then maybe just work on something else for a while. Or even better, multitask, and keep going back and forth between different projects. I'll often find that if I sneak off to work on my magical comedy of manners, I'll come back later to my grimdark post-apocalyptic novel about murder-chinchillas with a fresh eye and a new understanding of where that story needs to go next.

Even better if your cheating is a fling—like, if you go off and just write some flash fictions. Or noodle on something that you're not even sure is going to turn into a real project.

4) Make writing more of a communal activity

I *told* you we'd keep talking about community. Because it's everything.

Writing is usually kind of a solitary activity, involving a lot of staring at a blank screen or page, trying to make words appear. So it's essential to find ways to connect with other writers. Join a writing group, and swap critiques with other authors. Go to a writing class, or join a structured workshop like Clarion, Odyssey, or Viable Paradise.

But also, read your work aloud every chance you get—at open mics, at curated events, or on Instagram live. Post excerpts or entire pieces online, to share them with other people. Join support groups, Discord servers, or Slacks.

Nothing has done more to improve my writing than getting feedback from other writers, and watching people's faces while I was reading my work to them. But also, I don't think I'd still be here, and still writing, without my friends and that awareness that we're all in this together.

5) Find a routine, or a ritual

A good routine helps make the act of writing special, something to look forward to, when I'd probably rather be checking social media or playing video games.

When I started out, I would get off my day job and walk over to the neighborhood Coffee Bean and Tea Leaf with my refillable plastic travel mug and fill it with turtle mocha, then write for an hour or two at home, in a sugary over-caffeinated haze. Later, once I was working from home, I found a different routine: after my paying gig ended, I'd walk a couple miles to clear my head, ending at a cafe where I'd write until dinner.

When all the cafes in San Francisco shut down their indoor seating during the pandemic, I had to find a new routine—in fact, this was one of the main reasons I struggled to be productive. I finally came up with a new schedule: write at my desk at home during the day for as long as possible, then exercise in the evenings and then sit in bed, defacing a notebook in blue ink. Scribbling at bedtime helped me clear my head, and I could work on the secret project that I was cheating on my young adult novels with. Around that time, I noticed a number of writers on Twitter saying they'd started waking up an hour earlier to write.

Anything you can do to separate your writing time from your grout-scraping time, or your paying-the-bills time, is useful. Light a candle. Listen to a particular type of music. Sit in your garden. Hang out with your pet(s). Wear your special writing shirt. Whatever. It sounds silly, but it really helps me, and a lot of other people I know.

6) Take time to read something you love (or think you might love)

When I talk to writers who are skating on the edge of burnout, one thing often comes up: they don't have time to read anymore. And when I'm on a roll, or on deadline, I'll sometimes go for a couple weeks without reading, but then I start to fiend for it. I often feel like I can't make good wordstuff unless I'm feeding my brain some excellent words from other people.

I usually prefer to read stuff that's not too much like whatever I'm trying to write—and I'll cheat on books I'm reading, just as much as the ones I'm writing. I graze a lot. I'll have a superhero comic and a poetry book and a young adult fantasy and a literary epic and an anthology propped open next to my bed, slowly sacrificing their spines to my fickleness.

Even if you only ever want to write epic fantasy, your writing will benefit tremendously from reading every other genre, from romances to literary fiction to murder mysteries. Every genre has its own strengths that you can learn from, and you can stay connected to the thrill of writing by exposing yourself to the endless variety of word-bombs out there.

7) Reread something you wrote in the past that you're still happy with

This sounds egotistical, but it's just plain logistical. The times when I'm like "Ugh I can't do this" or "I hate my writing" or just "I don't know where the words go," I go back and just read a paragraph of something I wrote in the past, that I still like. Could be something I wrote last week, or something I wrote a year or two ago. This way, I can reconnect with my own writing voice, but also reassure myself that I, at least, like my own prose just fine. No matter how new or insecure you are, I bet there's a paragraph that you wrote and are proud of, and there's nothing wrong with going back and just basking in it for a moment.

Works in progress are so lumpy and misbegotten, sometimes it's nice to spend a moment with a finished product and go, "I made *this*." This is another reason to try and find spaces to share your writing, and read it aloud to people.

8) Change up how you write

Like I said above, a lot of my writing routine lately revolves around going back and forth between typing on my computer and writing longhand in a blank notebook. Those two modes of writing activate different parts of my brain, and feel like different processes—for one thing, it's harder to go back and edit what I already wrote, when it's in pen and ink. And writing in a notebook feels more personal, more like keeping a journal. Plus I can doodle. Doodling is magic! My story brain comes to life when I doodle, even if my art is generally not that great.

I've also been doing some writing—including bits of these essays—using speech to text, when I take long walks outside. If you're in a rut, sometimes it's worth throwing out your routine and writing in a whole other way.

9) Give yourself permission to just leave something broken for now

This is a huge one. You can easily get stuck throwing yourself at the same problem over and over, until you get sick of staring at the same few pages. And sometimes that's what you gotta do, if you can't see where the story goes after this point. But sometimes you can just skip over the broken bit and trust that you'll know how to fix it later.

Like I said back in chapter seven, eat dessert first! If there's a part of the story you're excited to write, write it NOW. Having that moment clear in your head (and on the page) will help you write everything that leads up to it. In the second book of my upcoming young adult trilogy, I wrote all the climactic scenes early on, and then I could see exactly where these people were going to end up as I was writing the choices that got them to that point.

10) Just write some moments, even if you're not sure where they go, or if they'll fit

Whenever I'm working on a project, I keep a separate document open that I call the "dump file." It's just a mishmash of cool moments, people speaking their truth, and actual poetry that I hope I'll be able to thread into the manuscript later. Sometimes I have a scene that I've already written down, but there's a cool line in the dump file that I can insert that just adds an extra spark. Sometimes it's fun to just write a bit from the point of view of someone who hasn't gotten a POV yet.

I often find that opening a new blank document and just free-associating is a great way to reconnect with the story I'm trying to tell, untethered from all the bones I've already laid down.

11) Never stop brainstorming

The other reason I often open a new blank document is to keep spitballing ideas for what's happening, and what might happen next. The more outlandish the ideas, the better. Sometimes the worst ideas provide the fertilizer that leads to excellent ideas later.

I often think about the advice a friend gave me: "You can't be too precious about any of your writing." She meant that you need to be willing to change things up, in response to feedback or editorial direction, or "studio notes." But I've started thinking of this as good advice in general: everything I've written down is temporary, up for grabs. And not being precious about it helps me to avoid taking it too seriously—which, see above about the road to burnout-ville.

Here's a fun tip: When you quit writing for the day, write down a list of five things that could happen next, from most to least likely. Chances are at least one of those things will hit you in a new way when you start up again.

12) Give yourself permission to feel crappy about your writing

You're going to hate your own writing sometimes. It's not the end of the world—or your writing life, for that matter. Everybody who writes has times when they loathe their own work.

Writer's block is a made-up thing that doesn't exist, but there are all kinds of reasons why you might be feeling stuck or unhappy. This may sound counterintuitive in a chapter about how to keep the fun in writing—but if writing isn't fun, or you're feeling bad about it, you should interrogate why. Don't feel ashamed or beat yourself up, but step back and think about what's going on. You could just be suffering from imposter syndrome or feeling overwhelmed by the state of the world, but there could also be something wrong with your story that you're not letting yourself see because you're determined to push forward.

I treat bad feelings like a diagnostic instrument. Including boredom and malaise. They might not tell you what's wrong exactly, but they can give helpful clues. You could be forcing yourself to write something you don't really believe in, and your gut is trying to tell you. I have never felt such a sense of relief as when I've switched from pushing forward to troubleshooting. Hurting yourself in the name of momentum is not fun.

Writing should be your happy place—and hopefully the above tips will help you to make it that way. But it's okay to feel bad sometimes, and acknowledging the bad feelings is the first step to getting your groove on again.

SECTION IV

—

WHAT WE WRITE ABOUT WHEN WE WRITE ABOUT SPACESHIPS

CHAPTER 17

■

How to Write a Political Story
Without Falling on Your Face

Every story is political, whether it's about war or boat racing.

We use narratives to create our sense of shared reality, and to provide a heuristic for the way the world works. Our assumptions shape every aspect of our writing, whether those assumptions are "you can always trust people in authority" or "meritocracy is a lie." Every book or short story excludes some details and incidents, and highlights others. Plus, as we've discussed, every author has an ideal reader in mind—and that imaginary consumer's level of privilege will shape each story's choices.

A lot of our most popular genre labels don't describe the stories themselves, so much as the affinity groups they're intended for. (See "literary fiction," "romance," "young adult," and "urban"—which, come to think of it, could all be used to describe the exact same book, with a different cover and text treatment. But that's a whole other essay.)

For my money, the most thrilling and entertaining stories are the ones that own their politics proudly. (Don't let anybody sell you any false dichotomy between "political" and "fun" storytelling!) But at the same time, it's important to think really carefully and deeply about the messages you're including and the assumptions you're making. And the story has to come first, natch.

Thanks to the internet and especially social media, we're all way more aware of the political meaning of stories than ever before. Everyone's accustomed to a torrent of think pieces, podcasts, tweets, and memes dissecting the meaning of stories.

(I may have helped to contribute a little bit to this flood, and I regret nothing.) Some of our hottest debates, among activists and actual politicians, revolve around TV shows, movies, and books.

In November 2016, I was working in a TV writers' room. The day after the election, we all straggled into work and gulped down instant oatmeal in the break room, trying to make sense of what had just happened. And then we sat down around our conference table and set about trying to figure out what all our carefully constructed plot points meant now, in this very different version of reality. Everyone in that room knew that our story had just changed dramatically—even though the actual incidents and moments were exactly the same as they were the day before.

History has a way of rewriting fiction without changing a word, which is why we talk so much about stories that have aged badly. You can't do anything to prevent this slippage. The only thing you can do is examine your story carefully—and strive to avoid falling into some of the biggest failure modes, like clunky metaphors, crude allegories, and rusty tropes.

Failure modes

Climate change is here, and it's real. I really believe that we need to be including it in our stories about the present and future, even if it's just in the backdrop or as part of the world-building.

But when I say "we need to write about climate change," people often picture something like *Captain Planet:* a delightful yet kludgy lecture in story form, in which polluters are literal cartoon villains. Or something where people stand around discussing tipping points and carbon sinks and snail habitats. Whereas my favorite climate stories are more like Sam

J. Miller's *Blackfish City,* or *Princess Mononoke*—rich, intense, with characters and worlds that feel urgently alive.

Similarly, a lot of people got their ideas about political allegory from the original *Star Trek,* in which black-and-white body paint and Muppet fur are used to deliver simplistic messages about the dangers of racism and proxy wars. The clunkiest sort of allegory, in which blue cat people stand in for real-life Indigenous people on Earth, is hard to avoid even if you're unaware of it—but this is one case where being aware of what you're doing is no excuse for making a mess.

I encourage you to hunt down K. Tempest Bradford's online essay "Androids and Allegory" about androids as an allegory for the "other"—and how this takes on a very different meaning when Black creators craft stories about androids who look like Black people, rather than the Extremely White androids that we see most of the time.

It's also easy—consciously or otherwise—to fall into a metaphor, in which a character goes through an unreal experience that provides an analog for real experiences. For a while there, fantasy stories were full of people becoming addicted to magic (like Willow in *Buffy the Vampire Slayer*), and at its worst, this often turned into a way of dramatizing a simplistic and judgmental view of real-life addiction. Television, movies, and other media are full of half-baked metaphors for disability, abortion, terrorism, crime, and other issues that affect real people's lives in the real world.

Another failure mode is the thoughtless thought experiment, like "What if we sent all the left-handed people to live on a space station and forced them to learn backward writing?" A good thought experiment allows us to look at a choice, or an ethical question, or an aspect of human nature, without all the clutter that real-life situations impose—and often, the "answer" is not easy or obvious. But a bad thought experiment feels as if a bunch of pieces were shoved into place, to force us to reach the conclusion the author wants us to reach.

As for tropes . . . we've all gotten way more trope savvy in the past decade or so, and everything that can possibly happen in a story has its own trope name—which, in turn, has helped us to realize that tropes are ubiquitous and inescapable. When we complain about tropes, what we're usually complaining about is a harmful metaphor, or thought experiment, embedded within the trope's nucleus. Like "bury your gays," or the aforementioned "smartest man in the room," or "manic pixie dream girl," to name a few major examples.

These tropes stack the deck of the world, to show that some lives are worth more than others, or to confirm the accuracy of stereotypes. Even if you're careful, you can easily allow tropes to push you around—this is the part of the story where the female character always gets captured and needs to be rescued—rather than making them work for you.

Like I said, just being aware that your story has a political meaning won't save you from falling into any of the above failure modes. You'll need to put in a little bit more effort to build something complex enough, and human enough, that the political meaning is both visceral and emotional. And to ensure that you're not creating a metaphor that will be hurtful to already hurting people.

Make it messy

Allegories and metaphors will show up, no matter what you do. A war story is always going to remind people of actual wars. Fictional enslavement will remind people of real enslavement. A tale of colonizing other planets can't avoid commenting on the history of settler colonialism here on Earth. You also can't help transforming your own experiences into signifiers—for example, even when I'm writing about cisgender people, I constantly find myself writing versions of the trans experience.

Once you accept this inevitability, you have an opportunity to examine more deeply what you're saying, intentionally or otherwise, about these real issues. You can also run the story past people for whom these issues might not be purely theoretical, like sensitivity readers. (We'll talk more about sensitivity readers soon.)

And then? Try to make your story so messy and human that it lives in people's heads and hearts, and they obsess about these characters and these situations—rather than seeing them purely as stand-ins for real-life people and things.

I worried endlessly about the witches and the mad scientists in *All the Birds in the Sky,* because I could see how the conflict between them could easily turn into a Gene Roddenberry–style allegory. The bad version would have featured witches who despise all technology and live in treehouses, eating nothing but lichen, fighting against scientists who wear excessively starched white tunics and goggles, and speak only in jargon.

That's why I went to such great lengths to complicate both sides—like, the coven leader Ernesto is a massive fan of his microwave oven, and all of the witches obsessively use the latest gadgets. (In a deleted scene, they all do karaoke.) When I was a teenager, I spent a summer living in a Buddhist temple in Taiwan with my best friend, and we were startled to see all the nuns toting cellphones and getting around on motorcycles, because we were expecting to see ascetics who had forsworn all modern appliances—and I think that was in the back of my mind when I was developing my witch characters. Meanwhile, the mad scientists are just regular hipsters, who sometimes engage in a lot of magical thinking.

The less clear-cut and simplistic the differences between the two sides were, the easier it was for me to buy into their conflict (and the allegory about science and nature at its heart) when matters came to a head.

When I think about the worst examples of "this stands in for this" in speculative fiction, there's often an oversimplified world or one-dimensional protagonist in the mix. The closer the story is to the real experience of being alive and trying to make sense of a muddled world, the less likely you are to end up with a "Frank Gorshin declaiming in body paint" situation. And as we were saying about emotion, details matter. If we can feel a character's itchy collar and smell the wet paint in their newly refurbished office, then we're more likely to buy into the reality of their situation instead of seeing it as pure metaphor.

The more you nail down the details of how things actually work, the less prone your world will be to follow metaphor-logic rather than story-logic. The mark of a truly terrible allegory is that the facts change to suit the meaning, rather than the meaning coming out of the facts. If you decide halfway through your story that anybody

WRITING EXERCISE: TAKE A TROPE (OR ALLEGORY) AND MESS IT UP

Here's a fun writing exercise: pick a trope, or an allegory. The trope could be something like "born sexy yesterday," in which a female-presenting person is somehow both childlike and overwhelmingly sexual. The allegory could be along the lines of "evil corporation wants to bulldoze the last forest to print brochures advertising a tree museum." (These are just examples—feel free to pick something different.)

Write down a short, one- or two-sentence description of how this trope or allegory would normally play out. Summarize the setup and the development—in the purest, simplest version, how would the situation be introduced, and how would it escalate? And then write a few words about why this trope or allegory might appeal to people.

Then let's take this idea and make it messy. Try to imagine what it would be like to be in the middle of that situation—

imagine yourself as the girl who's being sexualized in spite of being brand-new, or as the middle manager who's been entrusted with the job of destroying the forest. How does this person feel about their role in such an alienating scenario? Put yourself in the shoes of the person who's usually just an object for other characters to react to.

Then try to add some stuff to this character that complicates their situation. Maybe the evil forest-destroying capitalist can have some counterintuitive hobbies, like they play in a ragtime band on the weekends, or they crave super-spicy eggplant. Or they care deeply about some endangered birds whose habitat they're about to destroy. Give them traits that clutter up their otherwise one-note character, or that make them feel torn about their situation.

Finally, add some wrinkles to the situation itself—like, with the "born sexy yesterday" character, maybe she's unleashed on a world where people's taste buds start failing on their who gets a paper cut from the Cursed Broadsheet will have an evil finger, then we need to learn this before it becomes a thing. And we need to understand why people are still reading this rag, in spite of the "evil finger" problem. (I'm betting it's the recipes. It's always the recipes.)

Messiness and consistency sound like opposites, but they go hand in hand. Humans will bring our own individual neuroses to a consistent world, and a reliable set of constants will enable more variation at the margins.

When you realize that your story contains political signifiers, you can go in two different directions, or possibly both at the same time. You can sharpen those likenesses, until the meaning is unmistakable and salient—like, my mad scientists in *All the Birds in the Sky* are clearly "about" technological hubris and the notion that we should abandon a doomed Earth for other planets as soon as possible. But you can also add more fuzzy edges and outliers and exceptions and quirks, until things become less clear-cut. If you can manage to do both those things at once, then you're ready to party down.

When you're living through a historical nightmare, it's easy to feel as if the real world is becoming some kind of exaggerated metaphor, or thought experiment. During such times, we need starkly political fiction—but we also need the kind of resilience and hope that come from stories about real, breathing people grappling with tough situations.

"All stories are political" is another way of saying, "All stories are about people living in society." And that means that the more real and messy you can make both the people and the society, the sharper the politics will be.

thirtieth birthdays, and older people have to ask younger people to describe the flavor of food for them all the time. Make the world itself stranger and harder to summarize in a sentence.

Once you've done these extra steps, look back at your chosen trope/allegory, and see if its meaning has changed or expanded. And you never know—maybe you'll find a story you're interested in developing further.

CHAPTER 18

✦

Good World-building Shows How Things Could Be Different

Some of my earliest memories involve being saved from trauma by imaginary worlds. When I was a child, bullies noticed my mercurial flair and identified me as a proper target for every rust-speckled item in the bully toolkit. I got through elementary school and junior high by obsessively watching anime and space opera shows, but also by inventing more and more elaborate worlds in my head—both in games of Dungeons & Dragons and in my own scribbles. I constantly sketched maps of palaces, starships, monster forests, and superhero headquarters.

I was a world-builder before I knew anything about storytelling.

I still cope with stress and oh-shit-we're-all-gonna-die feelings by retreating into imaginary worlds of my own creation. I'm pretty sure I'm not alone. There's immense comfort in endlessly proliferating details. Every time the so-called real world gets worse, you can just add more complexity to your fantasy realm or galactic civilization, the same way the Winchester Mystery House kept adding more rooms. You can weave yourself a cocoon out of unreal real estate.

Speculative fiction authors love to talk about world-building. It always sounds super tough, like you should wear a hard hat and a safety harness, and use a protractor the size of a football field. But world-building is really just the process of inventing places and things that fictional people can interact with. You can't tell a story, in any genre, without world-building—even a "realist" story set in a small town has to establish the small town and its history—but world-building can be a pleasure in itself, rather than a means to an end.

You can use world-building to distract yourself during a never-ending catastrophe. But that same process can also help you (and others) imagine a path to liberation.

The best world-building contains the seeds of change, and allows us to see how things could be different. And conversely, a lot of mediocre world-building contains the unspoken message that "This is the way things are, just because. And there's no point questioning any of it." How things work is often not as interesting as how they *don't* work. And the ways that they should work, if things were better. And the way things used to work, until something went wrong (or right).

World-building grounds the story, shapes your characters, and makes their lives more complicated. And it's arguably the most political part of writing, because it's about systems. You're deciding the way things work in your world, but also the rules that your characters have to live by. These rules and systems include stuff your characters can't ignore—the same way you can't stroll onto a busy highway in the real world—but also the stuff they barely notice.

In real life, we all ignore stuff that's right in front of our faces. We step over homeless people on the street and tune out graffiti on bus shelters. The best world-building helps us to see the whole picture, including the people who've been shut out or stepped on. And the most basic everyday actions depend on complicated systems: you can't eat lunch without farms and some food-distribution apparatus, and the food you eat reveals something about your ecosystem. You can't go to the bathroom without sewers. And so on.

Food, in particular, is more complicated than it first appears. Many European staples came from settler colonialism in the

Americas—Italian cooking didn't have tomatoes, the British didn't have potatoes. Spam is considered a luxury food in South Korea, because US soldiers introduced this processed-meat treasure after World War II. Whenever you look at food, you'll see historical accidents that are weirder than anything fiction could devise.

World-building is dynamic rather than static

We tend to think of world-building and story as in opposition—like, the story happens to the world, or against the backdrop of the world. But world-building is made out of stories.

In a believable world, every item has its own origin story. If you throw a rock, you'll hit a choice somebody made in the past—and there's always the possibility they could have made a different choice. Never trust a world where nothing has changed for thousands of years, where things just "make sense," or where every aspect was dictated by purely utilitarian considerations.

That big staircase in front of City Hall? It's made of granite because there was a mayor fifty years ago who hated marble, and it's worn down on one side because these merchants decided to shlep a bunch of fake psychic orbs up those stairs, every day for years. Also, there's a half-finished war memorial out front, because we ran out of money and realized that particular war had been a mistake.

I get annoyed when everything in the present of a story is happening for reasons—but the past just "is."

When George Miller was directing *Mad Max: Fury Road*, he and cowriter Nick Lathouris came up with backstories not just for every character, but for "every vehicle, every steering wheel," he told *Vanity Fair*. Everything had a reason why it was the way it was, which gave the movie "its texture."

World-building reveals itself in crisis. I often think of the tip I heard from *Arctic Rising* author Tobias Buckell: instead of describing a room in a static fashion, like "there are three chairs and one of them has scalloped arms," you can use a fight scene to establish the physical space. For example, you can let people know about the chair with the scalloped arms by having someone knock it over in the middle of a brawl. The same is true on a larger scale. You can explore the world, in part, by showing it breaking. The only time you ever need to tear up the floorboards of your house and expose its guts is when the foundations are rotting.

Take *The Left Hand of Darkness* by Ursula K. Le Guin, a book that's like a masterclass in world-building. There's so much brilliant stuff, from folklore to mysticism to gichy-michy to cultural clashes to landscapes that feel downright immanent. But a big part of why it all works so well is that the world is already changing before Genly Ai shows up. Genly blunders into the middle of a situation where Gethen is in the middle of a crisis of modernity, in which Orgoreyn is becoming a nation-state and developing a theory of war.

We often think of traditions as ancient when they really go back about seventy years. Most of the "immutable" features of the Western world were invented either in the Victorian era or right after World War II. The harder people try to insist that something is "the way it's always been done," the more they're covering up the fact that they decided to do it this way after suffering some immense trauma. Wounded people crave the illusion of permanence, and so do people who've recently risen to power.

Even if you're only creating fake places to keep your mind off the toxic disasters around you, including a backstory will make the whole thing more fun. Think of it as a way of building in more layers of complexity—instead of just tacking on another

kingdom to the west, you can build past versions of the king-
doms you already have. Doing this will also help to chip away
at the inherent conservatism of a lot of world-building.

And once your world has a past, you can start to give it a
future.

A good world is worth fighting for—or fighting to change

The moment you start making up stories, you'll want to create
a place where people want to spend a lot of time. Because if
readers don't want to hang out in your floating mega-city, they
won't be nearly as interested in the people who live there. Most
writers obsess about creating a "sense of place." We even try to
turn places into a type of character, so that you can imagine
yourself having a relationship with these locales, and we try to
give them that lived-in feeling that lets people imagine that they
could hang out there.

That's why people spend so much time cosplaying and doing
fan art and trying to place themselves in Narnia, or Middle-
earth, or the Federation, or the world of *The Expanse*. These
worlds contain a host of details that let you imagine eating lem-
bas bread, or riding on a tauntaun, or hanging out in a grungy
space station full of Belters. Fictional languages, rules of behavior, carefully described spaces, and complex customs are all
ways to suck people into believing in the world, and wanting
to spend time there. The most successful world-building can be
aspirational.

Years of watching television have conditioned me to think
of this in terms of building a few standing sets. Take the show
Frasier: most of the action takes place in Frasier's apartment, his
favorite coffee shop, or his radio-station booth. This is a cost-
saving measure, but it also makes those three locations feel cozy

and familiar, and full of intimate details. So when I start a new story, I often try to construct a handful of locations that I'm going to give extra attention to.

Once you've fallen in love with a special realm that never existed, the next step is to build up a fierce yearning to make improvements. We naturally want to protect the places we love from being ruined, but that impulse can go even further, toward leaving the site better than we found it. All the structural injustices and abuses that you included in your world-building might seem fixable, if your characters just get off their butts.

Community is everything

Which brings me to another aspect of world-building that people often seem to overlook: community. A good world contains a sense of the communities that people belong to, rather than just placing a unique and fascinating individual alongside a faceless crowd. As I said before, nobody changes the world on their own.

I talked before about how writers need to belong to a community—

HOW TO MAKE MINOR CHARACTERS JUMP OFF THE PAGE

The more elaborate the world, the larger your supporting cast needs to be. Separate countries, cities, guilds, or bands might each require multiple people, depending on how much time we're spending with them. If you want the reader to care about the schism between two groups of fire-starters (the swamp-gas igniters versus the greeting-card burners), that means caring about some of their members.

Not every character can get pages and pages of development, or their own POV—so a really ambitious universe will require a small army of bit-players, to make everything legible.

The good news is, you can make a minor character pretty memorable in a few lines. Charles Dickens used to do it all the time: his novels are full of people who turn up now and then, and never wear out their welcome. He gives each minor figure a distinctive name ("Serjeant Buzfuz"), an unusual way of talking, a collection of tics and strange habits, a trenchant opinion or two, and a unique relationship to a more major character.

For a character we only see once or twice, I'll spend a bit of time trying to give them an odd habit, a memorable detail—or better yet, a contradiction. (A vegan who loves to go deer hunting is bound to stick in your mind.) Maybe their appearance can stand out in some way, like an unusual hairdo or a scar. I'll try to give a hint about their obsessions and preoccupations, so we know they have just as much of an interior monologue as everyone else.

There's nothing wrong with having the narrator, or another character, tell us interesting facts about a person whom we meet a few times. If Professor Thimbleswipe has never gotten over her doomed love affair with the Swan Queen, we don't need to learn about it straight from the professor's own mouth. As with real people, secondhand gossip is just as interesting as firsthand confessions.

but so do characters. Sure, your characters can reject the communities they come from, or have a thorny relationship with their roots. But when you think about the worlds we all wish we could go live in, they usually have one thing in common: strong groups, clubs, nations, cultures, affiliations, etc. That's true of *Twilight*'s vampires, the crew of the *Rocinante,* and countless others.

A truly rich world contains a lot of intersecting and conflicting groups, each with their own languages and habits and interests. I'm a sucker for stories about relationships between groups, as well as within groups. The popularity of "personality test" stories like *Divergent* and "secret society" tales like *Shadowhunters* proves that the notion of belonging someplace is a hell of a drug. Whenever I write about people searching for their own identity (which is pretty much all the time), I'm mostly talking about finding your people.

How do you write about community? By writing about people. A strong supporting cast should include multiple members of any affinity group that is meaningful to your protagonist, so we can learn the rules of that group from those folks. If different members of the same subculture disagree about fundamental aspects of their shared rules or ideals, so much the better.

I personally hate writing crowd scenes. If I have to write a moment involving more than two or three characters, I break out in hives. So the more I can do to establish a community through more intimate conversations, and individual relationships within the whole, the happier I tend to be. A community, in the sense of a crowd, can be mostly off-screen, or even physically absent the entire time, as long as we spend time with individuals who belong to it.

But also, none of those items you're including in your worldbuilding—the food, the buildings, the items of clothing—are cultureneutral. They all come from a group of people, or are claimed by a specific subculture or tradition, or else they're just props.

Communities don't just make world-building richer. They also provide allies, and motivation, in the struggle to make things fairer.

Dialogue is a huge tool for keeping your dramatis personae distinct. Every character should have their own way of talking, which tells you something about them as an individual, but also as a member of a group. Different cultures or subcultures will have their own unique turns of phrase, or patterns of speech, that mark their denizens as separate from everyone else.

I'll try lots of tricks to make different people speak differently—like having some characters speak mostly in sentence fragments while others speak in long run-on sentences. Or having some characters use more words with Greek and Latin roots, while others use more Germanic words. Or putting more em dashes into a character's speech (even if I take them out eventually). One character might always blurt out what they're feeling, while another might keep circling around the truth. I might also have one character who makes lots of definitive statements, while another speaks in hesitant questions. It's totally okay to give a supporting player a catch phrase, or a few unusual words that they're wont to use.

In case it wasn't obvious, there's no simple hack for creating character-specific dialogue. A lot of it comes down to thinking about the character and what's going through their head, and what reaction they're hoping their speech will elicit. I spend a lot of time listening to how real people talk, and I'll often read my dialogue out loud to make sure it sounds natural enough. I try never to have anyone speak perfect English, unless I'm writing a fussy or overeducated character.

When it comes to dialogue, most authors only really have a handful of "voices" that come naturally, myself included. I can always summon a cynical bad-ass, a neurotic overthinker, or a wide-eyed naif, for example. Beyond that, I make a huge conscious effort to keep changing things up. Ideally, you should be able to present a piece of dialogue with no speech tag, and the reader should know without being told who just spoke.

An imaginary city will always consist mostly of dummy build-

They're what we fight for, and how we fight for it.

That brings me to the final way that world-building is about (r)evolution: you never really finish building a world.

I usually find world-building needs to be done in several phases. I'll spend some time at the start of a writing project, trying to nail down enough context that I can write some scenes without my characters just sitting in a blank void—and making sure I have a setting that works with the story I'm hoping to tell.

Then I'll keep stopping as I write—because I can't write the nightclub scene until I figure out what nightclubs are like in this universe, or I can't figure out what happens next without fleshing out the ground rules. Picture a cartoon character walking down the street, and you keep drawing the sidewalk they're about to step on—that's how I often feel, in the middle of a project where I'm still filling in the details.

During revision, I'll go back and keep adding more layers of history and details, because the world still feels threadbare in spots. Or I'll realize there are holes in the story I've written, or something doesn't make sense, or I never explained a crucial thing (because I don't understand it yet myself). And while I'm adding layers and layers of history and everyday details, I'm also subtracting everything that makes no sense or breaks the rest of the world.

ings, with no walls or floors—but if you build it right, people will believe that they could walk through any front door and find something inside. The same applies to your supporting cast: you'll never be able to develop most of them, but you can leave people believing they're all the heroes of their own private stories.

Even after the book is published, I'll keep adding details to the world in my head. Readers will inevitably have questions that I can't answer unless I flesh out the world some more, or I'll write supplementary material. Or I'll just add to my own head-canon. The world-building really never stops, even if—god, I wish—I'm happy with every word on the printed page.

And that's the magic of world-building. It's endless, and transformative, and full of layers, in both time and space. That complexity can be a means of escape, but also a tool of revolution.

CHAPTER 19

The Unexamined Story
Is Not Worth Writing

The sixth episode of Netflix's *Baby-Sitters Club* has a scene that perfectly sums up my philosophy of writing. Claudia is displaying her Warhol-esque paintings of candies at an art show, and the judge startles her by asking what her artwork means to her. What was Claudia's motivation for these paintings, and what was she hoping people would take away from her images of Hubba Bubba? Claudia can't really answer. At last the judge says, "I would urge you to ask yourself why. Why this? Why now? Why me?"

Maybe that judge is supposed to be a mean jerk who's crushing poor Claudia's artistic dreams, but I found myself nodding and saying, "YES MEAN CAT-GLASSES LADY YES." Because those are the questions I ask myself all the dang time. If I had to choose between a writing day where I produced thousands of words, and one where I found more interesting answers to those questions about the story I'm working on, I'd pick the answers every time.

I used to be surprised when a Theme showed up in something I was writing. I'd be chugging along, and I'd notice a particular idea popping up in different contexts. And meanwhile a bunch of events in the story seemed to have connections that went beyond mere plot and causality. This felt like real magic. My story was becoming more than a collection of events and emotions and conflicts—it was *about* something.

Eventually, I started trying to make that thing happen on purpose. I thought about theme earlier in the process, and about what this story meant to me—without kidding myself that I could know what it would mean to someone else, later on.

Some people say that writers should never know what our own stories are about, and that it's up to readers and critics to tell us what our own work means later. But how stoned do those people think I am? (Okay, pretty stoned, let's be honest.) Meanwhile, a lot of writers seem scared to dig too deep into why they're doing this, to interrogate their own process, because they're worried they'll ruin the magic.

But for me, all the questioning and self-examination and brainstorming *is* the magic. I feel most enchanted by writing when I'm thinking deeply about the meaning of something I'm writing, and why I'm choosing to write this thing, instead of something else. The answers to those questions are often surprising, and they give rise to more complex questions and answers. Half the joy of writing, for me, comes from intentionality.

My best stories are usually the ones where I had a clear idea in my head of what I was exploring. Those are the stories where the plot and story, and the concerns of the characters, are tightly bound up with the narrative's thematic concerns. Likewise, as a reader, I get more wrapped up in a story that seems to have something specific on its mind.

Conversely, stories that I can tell were written without much introspection on the part of the author often feel mechanistic to me—things happen because they happen. The characters go through the motions, but none of it has much weight beyond the stakes of the plot.

When we talk about theme, you might think of something dry and abstract. Or dreadfully pat, like a fifth-grade book report that finds the theme of *Huckleberry Finn* was "friendship." (No shade to fifth-graders, or book reports.)

That's not what I'm talking about. When I say "theme," I mean something that grabs you by the throat and digs down to your hottest, most unprocessed emotions. Something that speaks to what you're living through right now. A good theme springs out of your personal obsessions and turns them into complex ideas, thrilling actions, or both. If the plot is the bones and the characters are the heart and blood vessels, the theme is the guts *and* the brain.

And you may ask yourself, how do I work this?

If you could read any of the early drafts of my novels or stories, your eyes would bleed. But also, you'd notice pages and pages of questions. And fumbling, confused answers. Any time I feel uninspired, I stop and give myself a gut check. I try to identify the things that are happening in the story that seem to point in an interesting direction. I also keep demanding, "What made me want to write about these people and these things in the first place?" What does all of this mean to me?

As I said back in chapter six, with the centaur bounty hunters, every premise can be written an infinite number of ways. And that means the "best" story ideas are the ones where I have to tease out the implications and find my own meaning.

If picking a story idea is a matter of going on a lot of first dates, then finishing the story means an ongoing relationship, in which it's helpful to keep asking, "What are we doing here?" The same way a romance gets sweeter the more you communicate with your loved one about your hopes and anxieties, I've always found that I bond more tightly with my work-in-progress by taking it apart in my head and asking, "What am I getting out of this?" That way, I can home in on the juiciest parts.

To me, this kind of ongoing self-examination is indivisible from brainstorming. In other words, I figure out what comes next in the story, or what the characters are likely to feel and do, by excavating deeper into my own intent as the author.

Conversely, if I know for sure what's coming next, I try to figure out why I landed on that, so I can make it count.

When I get stuck in the middle of a story, it's often because I haven't yet figured out what it's about. The toughest stories to revise are the ones where I lost my grip on the meaning of the story while I was writing it, where I just kind of drifted.

I almost never look back at the pages and pages of notes I've made, including all those questions and answers. They're there, if I really want to know "What the hell was I thinking?" But the act of writing down these obsessions and inspirations is still invaluable to me; it means the things that are in the back of my mind are now slightly closer to the front of my mind as I write.

This "gut check" involves keeping an eye out for a few things:

1. The personal stuff that I might be trying to work through. I obsess a lot about what real-life experiences I'm trying to capture (mine, or other people's) in my fiction. I might start out with a cool idea about a party girl who goes into space, but realize I'm actually writing about peer pressure, and friends who are bad influences. Or a fun/weird idea about someone who's haunted by her own ghost might turn out to be about depression, and the ways that anger and depression feed on each other in an endless spiral.

    I'm a firm believer that every story is really about something in the author's own life, or the lives of people the author is close to. Not that we have to turn our friends (or enemies) into fictional characters with the details changed slightly—I haven't done that, at least consciously, in years—but we capture the emotion and the visceral experience of living through something by projecting them onto something else. (Think of Jared Padalecki imagining his dead dog.)

At the very least, plugging into all that real-life emotion will help you bring some extra fire to the furnace.

2. Things that keep happening, or seem connected beyond pure causality. If something keeps happening in your story, you have two basic choices: you can tweak things to make them less repetitive, or you can double down and make this a motif. Obviously a lot depends on what we're talking about, but the "motif" thing is often the better choice. As long as the reader can tell you meant to do this, and it's either a feature of the world or a set of parallels that you're creating consciously, then they'll go with it.

    Patterns create meaning—so the more clearly drawn and vivid the patterns in a work of fiction, the more meaningful it'll feel.

    Maybe you have a world where it's common to get kidnapped and put into cryo-sleep, because there are gangs that make a lot of money collecting cryogenic ransoms. Or the fact that two different characters get cryo-napped comes as a result of the choices they've made, in which they consciously chose to risk cryo-napping. And the differences between their cryo-napping experiences reveal something about who they are as people.

3. The characters' own obsessions. This is often the richest vein, for me. The things that float to the surface of the characters' internal monologues are, by definition, close to the story's heart. We care about protagonists who care about stuff— who crave answers to their questions, want to save someone

or something, or need to resolve an identity crisis. Anything the characters keep arguing about or trying to make sense of automatically appears at the center of the story's "tag cloud" of meanings.

You probably won't ever find The Answer as to what a story means and what's making you write it—but a lot of the fun of writing is trying to figure out what this story is saying to you, and how to make it speak louder.

How aware should the reader be of a theme?

Your own ideas and inspirations and themes don't necessarily need to be signposted in big letters for the reader. Often, the subtler the better, especially if you're trying to avoid a capital-A Allegory. It's just like any other aspect of creative writing: most of the work you do is under the surface, and maybe 10 percent is fully visible to other people.

That said, I'm a big fan of books that I can tell are about something—where people argue about ideas and ideals. When characters have a spirited philosophical discussion, I get pumped and start paying more attention. If two characters have a running debate that crops up every time they get together, so much the better. As a geek myself, I like characters who geek out. I also like characters (and narrators) who throw out aphorisms and words to live by—and judging from the popularity of discursive authors like Terry Pratchett and Robert A. Heinlein, I'm not alone.

But for me, the authorial obsessions underlying a piece of fiction come out in a bunch of subtler ways. Including the inanimate objects the author chooses to describe, and how. The plot devices and bits of world-building that feel most solid. The mistakes the characters make, and the dubious lessons they learn

FIND THE EMOTIONAL CORE OF YOUR STORY

Because a work of fiction is not an essay, I try hard to figure out what the emotional core of the story is—the source of the zappiest zaps of feeling and connection—and then I keep coming back to that core as much as possible.

The emotional core is the thing the characters care most about (and hopefully the readers will, too). Often, that's one relationship or cluster of relationships. Or the stake(s) that the characters will live and die for. The whole tale revolves around this core—and its high-voltage charge can help to light up all your obsessions and preoccupations underlying the story.

For example, in the wonderful *Legendborn* by Tracy Deonn, Bree is obsessed with finding out the truth about her mother's death, but over the course of the book this turns into a larger quest to discover who she is, where she comes from, and which world she belongs in. Bree's obsessions power the

from them. A million little choices that shape the structure, but also the texture, of the narrative.

You can't control what your reader cares about, or what meaning they decide to take away from your story, but you can control what you put energy into as a storyteller.

The wider ideas in a story don't have to map exactly onto all of the twists and turns of the plot, and it's often better if these two things are in conversation with each other. A story where plot and theme go on exactly the same lines tends to be overly simplistic, but a story where the plot keeps darting in and out of contact with the theme can feel rich and complicated. You can have moments that feel thematically loaded, in between moments of just solving an immediate problem or trying to get someplace.

And like I said about relationships, signifiers and symbols tend to get less powerful the more of them you have.

My favorite thing when I'm writing (or reading) is to feel as if the story is slowly getting deeper into a particular cluster of ideas and revealing more as the layers pull away. There's often a moment where a story gets far enough into a running discourse to reveal that things aren't what they appeared: opposites aren't really opposites, an insoluble question has a loophole, and you can see the deeper connections that unite what seemed to be disparate threads. I live for that shit.

And if you're worried about accidentally writing a cruddy allegory (or a fifth-grade book report about friendship) instead of a living, breathing story, I'm pretty sure a conscious focus on your own intent and preoccupations will help rather than hurt. Being aware of the things you're drawing on, and consciously trying to weave them into your story, will make you less likely—not more—to produce something that shoves its capital-T Theme in the reader's face with the subtlety of a neon-bright banner.

book and keep her pushing forward through countless trials, battles, and microaggressions. And as her quest for answers becomes more of an identity crisis, it illuminates the book's ongoing preoccupations about privilege, Arthurian lore, secret societies, and the legacy of slavery and Jim Crow. These concerns come out of character and story rather than ever feeling imposed from above, and it's beautiful.

The moments that make you cry, lead to your cast of characters doing something reckless and unexpected, or bond you to your heroes in a deeper fashion come out of the emotional core. The person or place or object that people will risk everything for, that's enshrined in the craggiest corner of their souls—that's what keeps a story humming with life. If you know what you're obsessing about *and* what your characters care about more than anything, then you're on your way to creating something that will shatter a lot of hearts and minds.

CHAPTER 20

Weirdness Gives Me the Strength to Keep Going

Scary times have changed the way that I think about weirdness. I used to think of strange and surreal art as a siege weapon—a cannon aimed at the walls of conformity, structural oppression, and well-of-course-ness.

But lately? I think of strange art as a source of reassurance and safety. A cozy blanket made out of nice fuzzy WTF.

Let me back up slightly. Tons of my favorite creators—from Philip K. Dick to Christopher Durang to Kathy Acker to George Clinton—have one thing in common: their work is gleefully, obnoxiously off-kilter. I grew up on *The Phantom Tollbooth,* Monty Python, *Krazy Kat, From the Mixed-Up Files of Mrs. Basil E. Frankweiler, Little Nemo,* and classic slapstick and monster movies, so I never had the slightest doubt that bizarre is beautiful.

A major reason why I wanted to become a writer was to see how far I could go. I had a near-limitless supply of gonzo story ideas, and I wanted to throw the absurdity of our world in everyone's face. I took it for granted that surreal art and fiction are closely linked to satire, and that over-the-top exaggeration was the best way of getting at the truth behind our flawed perceptions. In other words, surrealism is realer than "realism."

So my early short fiction was full of exploding cactus codpieces, sewer monsters that control the advertising industry, a wig haunted by the ghost of a drag queen, and genderqueer okra. I crammed as much incongruity into every page as 12-point

Courier New would allow, firing volleys of pure unreality into a world that was suffering under the delusion that it made sense.

Carol Emshwiller once wrote that the motive for most of her wondrously strange fiction was "estranging the everyday," and I feel that so deeply.

As a young writer, I drew courage from the ferocity of Bruce Sterling's landmark "Slipstream" essay, which called for writing that defied both genre and realism. I prowled through used bookstores looking for every book on the essay's "recommended reading" list, and got about as far as the letter C. I barely remember Madison Smartt Bell's *Waiting for the End of the World* (except that a kitten dies in an unforgivably cruel fashion), but John Barth's *Giles Goat-Boy* became an indelible favorite. Katherine Dunn's *Geek Love* was published a smidge too late to appear on Sterling's list, but it became a wellspring that I keep going back to.

Especially after I moved to San Francisco and transitioned, I found a community of people who were being outrageous in real life, and it made me want to go even further in my writing. I became part of a whole scene of Dada performance artists, zinesters, pranksters, queer rebels, and wild poets. I created a site called GodHatesFigs to satirize the notorious hate site GodHatesFags, and helped to organize events like the Ballerina Pie Fight.

When did I grow up and tone down the strangeness in my fiction? I didn't.

My stories are still full of cat butter and talking animals—but I think I got a skosh better at suspension of disbelief, so you're (hopefully) lured into believing that these utterly wack events are really happening to someone. And I never stopped feeling as if madcap silliness could be a wake-up call for people who are snoozing through a million-alarm fire.

Except that when things get really bad—like, everything is broken to the point where the entire world is made out of bloody shards—then a couple of things happen:

1) The absurdity and illogic of our institutions become painfully apparent, and nearly satire-proof. We hardly need a story about the Queen of Hearts shouting "Off with her head!" and explaining that words mean whatever she wants them to mean, when our actual leaders say similar things in public, every day.

2) I start to find immense comfort in any reminder that the world is intrinsically a bonkers place where anything can happen, including joyfully outlandish acts of resistance and liberation. I've talked a lot in these chapters about how the first thing the oppressors want to do is constrain your sense of what's possible—and a truly odd piece of art can loosen the stays on your corset, allowing you to breathe freely. Weirdness also reminds us that we can be our authentic, outrageous selves without being smushed like a bug.

So I have not deviated from the path of goofballery, but I have started to think of its purpose in different terms: as a source of consolation to myself, and possibly others, when everyone is near-inconsolable.

The unreal can be a saving grace

It's painful to have to pretend that the world makes sense, especially when doublespeak has become mainstream discourse. Orwell would plotz if he had somehow lived to see a world where "free speech" has come to mean "I want to silence my critics." So how do you use nonsense to protect yourself from nonsense?

Recognize that "strange" doesn't have to mean "ugly." A saving grace in recent years has been the renaissance (in the West) of cute weirdness—in cartoons like *Adventure Time*, comics like *Squirrel Girl,* and movies like *Guardians of the Galaxy.* Baby Yoda is adorably odd, and I'd argue so are Deadpool and Harley Quinn. Maybe "grimdark" has given way, slightly, to "sweetweird."

You might find it easier to take solace in the weird if you think of it as cuddly, or kind. Especially when "normal" means "hateful," as it so often does. Maybe try writing about cute robots, or baby dragons, or fuzzy monsters, who make up for their illogic with an abundance of gentle niceness.

But "ugly" is cool, too. So is gross. And nasty. Body horror can be a place to put all your darkest fears about loss of bodily autonomy, or a way to think about your relationship to your own idiosyncratic body. There's something incredibly freeing about letting all the shit hit the fan—literally—and imagining what comes next.

Chaos can be a balm to anyone who feels powerless. When you're not in control over vital aspects of your own life, it can be reassuring to imagine—or remember—that nobody else has a handle on it, either. There's a reason why post-apocalyptic stories are one of the most common forms of escapism.

A lot might depend on what you're seeking comfort from. Too much pressure? Try telling stories about irresponsible randomness. Scary danger and chaos? Maybe lean into the cartoon-logic that allows people to skateboard across the Grand Canyon without a scratch. And if it's the doublespeak thing, then pure gibberish can be an inoculation.

Satire is cool. I know I said a truly horrendous situation is nearly satire-proof, but it's always possible to go so far over the top that you can look down on the uber-jerks, and maybe drop some anomaly bombs on them.

Find the logic in logorrhea. Nonsense has a way of redshifting into sense, if you keep going far and fast enough. Especially when there are recognizable human beings in the middle of it,

WRITING EXERCISE: CREATING BELIEVABLE PEOPLE IN UNBELIEVABLE SITUATIONS

I've been teaching a workshop for the past few years called "Creating Believable Characters in Unbelievable Situations." The gist of it is that the more outrageous the events of a story are, the more grounded and understandable the characters might need to be—with a ton of caveats, like there are times when a cartoon character can exist in a cartoon world, natch.

As long as the reader believes in the characters, and the characters believe in the world, then the reader will believe in the world, no matter how clownpants the world might be.

So here's an exercise: write down a short description of a wild-and-woolly situation, like "being chased by cupcake robots through a city made of cake."

Now let's start coming up with the character who's in that situation. Write down at least one of the following:

which we'll talk about in a moment. Spend enough time spinning out non sequiturs, and eventually you'll find yourself making connections and associations between them, because that's just how brains work. We find patterns in anything, and all that loopitude suddenly makes a higher kind of sense. It's a game, sort of.

That's maybe the most reassuring thing about a scrambled narrative, especially when the world is a mess: there's meaning in everything, even the apparently meaningless. And the clues are there, if you look carefully at whatever you've laid down. You throw all your cards up in the air, and they'll land in some kind of order. Every time.

Things don't have to make sense to be safe, but it's nice to know that there's sense to be made, if you just look long and hard enough.

How to suspend disbelief in a truly odd story

Weirdness is a function of expectations, which in turn are a function of genre. Aliens showing up and eating everything in sight might be a jarring event in a work of mimetic "realism," but nobody will bat an eye if aliens turn up in a science fiction story. A toga at a toga party has a different meaning than a toga at a business meeting. Context also matters, which is why the makers of *Doctor Who* decided in the early 1970s that a yeti sitting on the toilet in Tooting Bec was more alarming than a yeti wandering the tundra.

So believable weirdness is, in part, a matter of setting and managing the reader's expectations, and recognizing the preconceptions the reader will bring to your chosen genre (or genre mash-up). If you really want to startle people, you need to set the table—and then yank the tablecloth off. Which means that there might need to be clear rules, or a sense of status quo, before the mayhem gets going.

And that brings us back to the characters—as I said in the section on believable characters in unbelievable situations, we need to understand what the characters think the rules are, and how those rules are being violated by all this chicanery.

Final thought: it's important to remember that weirdness can be

1. A grounded detail, like this person's favorite candy, or a pet peeve.
2. Something interesting about their backstory that might relate to this misadventure.
3. A sensory detail, like their feet hurt from running, or they feel sick to their stomach.
4. A personal goal, or obsession, that doesn't just relate to solving this immediate problem.
5. How does this situation make sense, or feel normal, to them? How do they explain it to themself?
6. What emotional toll are these events taking on them? Are they freaked out, or exhausted, or traumatized, or energized?
7. What position do they occupy in this world? How much power do they have?

Once you have one of each of those items, go back and write a paragraph about the situation you came up with earlier, integrating each of the character-specific items you brewed up. Ideally, the seven (or more) details will help the bizarre situation feel realer, and more believable, and you'll be closer to having a character you want to spend time with. Bonus points if your protagonist is a bit contrary, or even obnoxious, in the face of all this madcapitation, rather than just trudging meekly through the weirderness.

If your characters feel like people you could meet on a subway, you're at least halfway to suspension of disbelief. (Then you just need shock absorbers of disbelief, and maybe brake pads of disbelief.)

both offensive and defensive. A Molotov cocktail and a soothing elixir, at the same time. To utterly misquote Hunter S. Thompson, when the going gets weird, the weird become paladins.

CHAPTER 21

When Is It Okay to Write About Someone Else's Culture or Experience?

I still remember when I was scratching at the door of science fiction and fantasy, desperately trying to get noticed. I racked up piles and piles of rejections, but I just kept scribbling in obscurity (and Starbucks). And then I came up with a book idea that was absolutely guaranteed to put me on the map.

I was going to write an Asian-inspired epic fantasy novel.

I felt pretty qualified to write such a book. I'd been an Asian Studies major in college, and had become fluent in both Mandarin and Japanese. I'd lived all over Asia, working as a journalist in Hong Kong and studying at Beijing University. And I had a pretty fantastic idea, based on the *Kojiki* and the *Nihon Shoki*, two foundational texts in Japanese culture that are just bursting with fantastic story seeds. I was getting that thing I keep talking about in these essays, where I was falling in story-love and having tiny epiphanies every time my hands touched a keyboard. It felt like magic.

At the time, science fiction conventions were full of panels advising us White writers to go ahead and write about other cultural traditions. There had been a few too many fantasy novels based on the same Western European traditions, and everybody was hungry for something new and different. And just look—there was this amazing wealth of stories and traditions just waiting, outside of our own cultural heritage.

So I had high hopes that my Japanese-influenced fantasy

novel would finally get me in the door of mainstream genre publishing. I worked steadily on it, doing loads of research on the latest archaeological discoveries about ancient Japan—what people wore, what they ate, how they lived.

And then . . . I started getting that three a.m. stomachache. You know the one. The little anxiety spike in the wee hours that usually tells me that I'm trying to do something I'm going to regret, possibly for a very long time.

Here's the thing: I had seen firsthand how much my Asian friends were hurt by the flood of books by White people appropriating Asian cultures in the 1990s and early 2000s. We'd all rolled our eyes over *Memoirs of a Geisha,* but there were literally dozens of other books. Europeans were obsessed with Asian culture, but we kept coming back to the dream/pastiche of Asian culture that we'd made for ourselves, ever since *The Mikado* and Ezra Pound's laughable "translations" of Asian poetry. The turn of the millennium was full of Asian culture without Asian people, as everyone copied anime series and Tsui Hark movies without bringing along actual Asians.

Plus, after college, I had spent a few months working at a doomed Asian-interest bookstore near Harvard Square. I'd always tried to steer my White customers to books about Asia by actual Asian authors, without much success. These customers seemed to crave the comfort of a White author who could hold their hand and lead them through an unfamiliar culture. Even—especially!—when the book was from the POV of an Asian character. I got sick of ringing up stacks of Asia-focused books by European authors, most of which were cheesy or worse, and I started to dread going to work.

So I wrestled with my conscience for a while. I tried to convince myself that my Asian-fantasy project would be different. I was going to be careful! I knew what I was doing!

And then . . . I reluctantly decided to put that novel draft in a drawer. And then light the drawer on fire.

A short while after I put away my Asian fantasy novel, I started to write fiction and personal essays about my own experiences as a trans woman. There was a whole scene of trans and genderqueer and gender-nonconforming creators, all of us writing about our experiences of becoming our brightest truest selves and dealing with harassment and setbacks. We gathered in coffee shops and bars and bookstores, reading stories and poems and excerpts from novels, and it felt like we were inventing a whole new language to talk about our changing bodies and hearts.

And I found the same thing, from the opposite side: there were plenty of stories being published and filmed about trans experiences, but they were largely being created by cis people. I'm sure these books and movies did a lot of good and helped educate cis people and help them feel more comfortable with trans people's existence—but trans creators were mostly shut out. Especially when it came to fictional portrayals of trans people.

The more I thought about it, the more it seemed as though this was another example of what I'd seen in my bookstore job: cis people wanted cis creators to make them feel "safe" visiting the "exotic" realm of transness. They wanted a tour guide.

Representation without appropriation

So whenever I think about the ongoing (and constantly shifting) debates over cultural appropriation, I think about that "tour guide" thing. People from the dominant group will always seek out a non-challenging version of any marginalized group's experience, and it's easier to get that from authors who come from that same dominant group.

Privileged people can become conditioned to expect only one

type of story about a marginalized group, to the point where they won't accept any other stories, no matter how real.

So I've tried to strike a balance in my own work, when I write about marginalized people whose experiences are different from my own. I aim for representation without appropriation.

For example, even though I threw away that Asian-influenced fantasy novel, I've still included plenty of Asian characters in my fiction, including some pretty major characters. And I've definitely drawn on my knowledge of Asian history and folklore here and there. If I was writing about an alien invasion, some of the heroes fighting off the slime-flyers would probably be of Asian descent. And I'd do my best to give them the same inner life that I try to imbue all my characters with—including all the weight of culture, history, and lived experience.

But I've never tried to write stories that center uniquely Asian cultures or experiences. Like, I wouldn't try to write a story that's all about what it means to grow up in a Taiwanese family. Or a story about the experience of living through the Hong Kong protests from the point of view of a Hong Kong native. Or a deep dive into Chinese history. There are other people who could write those stories way better than I could.

That's where I decided to draw the line for myself, but everybody has to figure this out themselves. (And Hiromi Goto's 2014 WisCon guest-of-honor speech includes a very helpful checklist of questions to ask yourself before writing a story about a culture outside your own.) I feel like this is always going to be messy, and ever-shifting, and contain exactly no straight lines, because we're talking about human beings, and the complexities of history. You never get to be done trying to figure this stuff out.

The book world is slowly getting more inclusive—too slowly—but we still have a long, long way to go. And as long as the writing and publishing scene continues to reflect the huge power imbalances in the wider world, those of us with privilege need to stay mindful, and refuse to take on that "tour guide" role, ever.

It's also on us to do whatever we can to promote marginalized authors, and support them in telling their stories about their lived experience and their heritage.

But at the same time, all fiction, including fiction by people from the dominant group, needs to represent the diversity of the real world. It's essential for White authors, in particular, to include BIPOC characters in our work and to make them as recognizable and believable as any other characters. We all need to populate our worlds with people from many backgrounds, genders, sexualities, and disability statuses, *without* trying to tell the stories that aren't ours to tell.

Representation without appropriation is not an end state, but rather an ongoing process. Like many aspects of writing, it's a ton of work, a process that never becomes easy or clear-cut—but the work pays off, in richer characters and smarter story-telling. When I write someone who comes from a very different place than me, in terms of culture or marginalization, I feel a huge responsibility to get it right, but I also feel like this story is going to sparkle more, in the end.

Research research research

The good news is, there are a lot of resources out there to help us to strike that balance. The award-winning badass Nisi Shawl cowrote a fantastic book called *Writing the Other* (with Cynthia Ward) and is now running online workshops on writing about other cultures and experiences, with K. Tempest Bradford and a host of other teachers. There are also a ton of great resources on anti-racism and decolonizing science fiction.

When I set out to write somebody whose life is radically

different from my own, I do a lot of extra research—especially if this is a major character in the story. I'll get stacks of books from the library or the local bookstore, and do a deep dive into both history and sociology. I'll watch a hundred videos on You-Tube, plus movies and TV shows. And I'll interview actual living people about their life experiences—and I will pay them for their time, either in money or in donations to the nonprofit of their choice.

Even if my work touches on ancient history or folklore, I know that it connects directly to the people who are alive today. When you write about the future, you're really writing about the present—and I believe the same is true when you write about the past. So even if you're touching on ancient Chinese history, you need to understand how Chinese people in the twenty-first century think about their own heritage, and what it means to them. The past is always alive in the present, and the stories we tell about it matter.

I've talked before in these essays about how difficult it is to create characters who feel like real people, rather than stick figures or plot devices. I've learned the hard way that this becomes way more difficult when I'm writing about people who have had way different journeys through the world than mine. I'm not just talking about writing stereotypes—though, yes, I've written plenty of stereotypical characters. (And I've been lucky that people have mostly called me on them before those stories saw print.) But it's a more global problem than that.

I have a general tendency to write flat, lifeless characters, and yet trick myself into thinking I've written living, breathing individuals. And the more different those characters are from myself, the worse this issue seems to become. Simply put, I have a harder time getting into the head of someone whose life is very different from mine, which means I have to work harder, but also be constantly aware of this problem.

You don't know what you don't know—so it's hard to realize when you're missing something important.

And it's not enough for me to give a character an Asian name, and then pat myself on the back for representing Asian people in my fiction. The best fictional characters have a lived-in quality. This means they're shaped by everything that they've been through, and that includes all of the experiences that come out of their own identities. So even though I don't want to tell a story that would be better told by an Asian person, I'm always aware that I can't truly represent people from a marginalized group if I leave out the joys and challenges they share.

For example, I've learned the hard way that when writing BIPOC characters, I can't be afraid to show them facing structural barriers, or to portray their connections to their own communities. I won't shy away from depicting the garbage they've had to deal with as part of their marginalization, hopefully without descending into misery porn. In the case of my story "Clover," I found that when writing about a gay Egyptian man in North Carolina, I had to show how homophobia and Islamophobia had affected him, otherwise he wouldn't feel like a real person. And that meant talking to plenty of my friends whose experiences could help me illuminate those things for myself.

I screw up constantly, and the only thing I can do is try to do better and to be aware of my own shortcomings as an author— and all the ways that my privilege makes me worse at writing other perspectives.

And that's why I'm so utterly grateful for sensitivity readers. For years, I was asking my BIPOC and disabled friends to read my fiction and give me a gut check on how I was handling characters who were closer to their experience than to mine. When I first learned about sensitivity readers, I was overjoyed that there was a phrase to describe the thing I'd been asking people to do (and in some cases, that I had been doing for others), but

I was also embarrassed that I hadn't been paying people for that work.

And you don't even have to wait until your book is finished and polished to get some helpful input. As I mentioned, you can start talking to people early on, as part of your research. But you can also hire a developmental editor, who will work with you on your story and your characters earlier in the process, to make sure you're not going in a direction that you'll end up regretting.

Even when I've written White trans characters, I've made a huge effort to show those stories to other trans people, just to make sure I'm not inadvertently reproducing hurtful stereotypes or ideas about my own community. My own trans identity does not guarantee that I'll know what might prove hurtful to other trans folk—and in fact, this has sometimes happened, especially in the stuff I wrote early on in my career.

So where is the line between representation and appropriation? It's never an easy question, nor should it be. But I've found that a lot of soul-searching, and a willingness to listen, are key parts of reaching the former without straying into the latter.

A few years ago, I attended a panel at the Brooklyn Book Festival where Nelson George and Jeff Chang talked about cultural appropriation in music, and this helped shape my views on appropriation in fiction. In a nutshell, they said musicians who acknowledge where they've gotten their sound from, and who make sure the originators of that sound get paid, are less likely to be appropriating.

In the book world, too, it's important to think about those two things: respect and money. Who's getting them, and who deserves more of them? In other words, support marginalized authors, especially BIPOC authors. Promote their work, celebrate them, help them—and most of all, pay them. There is no substitute for actual inclusion of marginalized voices, at every level. And *never* fall into the trap of thinking there should only be one token author or voice representing a whole community.

Stories only matter because they're connected to people. There's nothing more tragic than when someone's story is present, but the person who actually lived that story is still locked outside.

SECTION V

■

HOW TO USE
WRITERLY TRICKS
TO GAIN
UNSTOPPABLE POWERS

CHAPTER 22

·

Find Your Voice and Make It Loud

People get terribly macho when they talk about writing style, or craft. They speak as if these are serious, austere matters—as if you need to put on thick gloves and a welding faceplate, and break out your spirit level, to make sure everything is absolutely plumb. Creative writing has been burdened with a lot of excess manliness, thanks to the twentieth century's glut of White men with exuberant facial hair, and this leads to the use of words like "sturdy" and "muscular" to describe prose.

So here's another way of looking at it: your writing style is a nice snuggly blanket, embroidered with pretty flowers, that will keep you safe and warm when the world is a cold and inhospitable place. You may start singing to yourself, in a soft voice, while you're wrapped in that blanket, and that song, too, is part of your writing style. Your distinctive use of words and phrases—your voice—can be a very reassuring thing to nurture in yourself.

Of all the ways you can use storytelling to get through a nasty time, developing your own voice as a writer is probably the most important. A lot of the essays in this book have been about how to talk to yourself (or your imaginary friends), but honing your voice will help you *listen* to yourself. You can remind yourself who you are, and that your voice, in particular, is vital and indispensable. You *can do this,* and in fact you already are doing this.

So much of storytelling is just a matter of finding the right words—the chains of meaning that carry the reader along from scene to scene, from image to image. Not the right words according to some luxuriously bearded icon, but the right words for the story you've set out to tell.

Style is, well, stylish. It's the most fun-loving, frivolous aspect of writing (at least when it's working and you're not screaming death-metal lyrics at a blank screen). When we talk about craft, or voice, we're talking about word tricks: games, metaphors, images . . . the notes of that song you're singing. We're also talking about doing the best job you can of getting the stuff in your head onto the page, in a way that represents you. And using each little word to create a sense of forward motion in your mind, and the mind of anyone else who reads your stuff.

I'm a big fan of wordplay, with an emphasis on "play."

Different people will have different ideas about what a "good" writing style looks like. Some people adore prose that's loaded up with lots of imagery, and liberally uses adjectives and adverbs and galloping gallimaufry. Other people think the only good writing is spare, with no ornamentation or unnecessary words whatsoever. Plus, what's considered "good" changes over time: back in the day, everyone was supposed to write like Raymond Carver, the famous minimalist. Then Dave Eggers' wry, confessional, looptastic sentences became everyone's role model.

People hate on adverbs, but I quite like them sometimes, actually.

But basically, any prose style that works, works. And by "works," I mean that the words say what you wanted them to say, they don't confuse or distract the reader from what matters, they keep the reader moving forward from sentence to sentence, and you can look back at your work and go, "Hey, I wrote that."

Writing is the only machine where there is no distinction between gears and ornamentation. Everything you put on the page is doing work and (hopefully) looking pretty. Looking pretty will make the work go better, and vice versa.

I was a prize-winning dancer, so you should listen to me

I was a dance champion in high school. No, really.

I used to do this dance that involved moving my feet very quickly, and just kind of scooting around—I did not move any part of my body from the ankles up, but my feet were unstoppable. My friends used to call this my "space-clearing dance." Maybe because people thought this dance was funny, or because I was clearly putting a lot of energy into it, I usually won a prize whenever they would have a dance contest at a high-school dance.

When I was a little older and started going to nightclubs, parties, and concerts, I started moving my hips and my arms and my shoulders, and basically my body.

I mention this because I feel like that's a similar journey to the one that I've taken with my writing style. My writing style started out energetic but repetitive—there were lots of words, and some of them were very good words, and I was laying them down with a lot of excitement, but I was using the same few tricks over and over. Even more than the singing metaphor I used above, I do think writing is a lot like dancing: every dance move helps to tell a story, and a good dancer can make you feel the music as well as hear it. All of that gyration and shaking adds up to something bigger.

My writing style improved as I learned to think in terms of scenes and capture real emotion. But also I expanded my repertoire of dance moves by experimenting and thinking more deeply about what I wanted my prose to do, beyond just make people laugh or scratch their heads. Experimenting with prose style is the key to getting better and keeping things fresh.

For a few years, I tried leaving out any words that weren't totally necessary. For example, does the verb "to fall" really need to be followed by the preposition "down"? I worked hard to minimize my use of the verb "to be," and to avoid having sentences begin with "It," or "There was." I weeded out turns of phrase that I'd seen a million times before, like "butterflies in my stomach" or "like a stuck pig." (What did that pig ever do to you?) I have been amazed at how often I can take a whole rambly paragraph and boil it down to a few words.

At the same time, I consciously tried to add extra words that I thought made my writing feel more conversational. Like, I have an addiction to the word "like." And "even," and "just." I will often include little word-flutters, to try and make my prose feel more like human speech, and less like something coming out of a text-synthesizer. One of my goals for my writing was warmth and friendliness, which don't necessarily come from stripping out every unnecessary word to create some hard skeleton of verbiage.

Sometimes words can just add a bit of texture, rather than meaning. Also, sometimes using a word slightly wrong, or picking an obscure and strange word instead of the most obvious one, can make the writing feel a bit more salubrious.

Here are a couple of experiments I tried in recent years. When I was revising *The City in the Middle of the Night*, I took any sentence that had a metaphor or any sort of imagery, and made it a separate paragraph. This forced every image to stand on its own, rather than hiding behind a wall of prose, and made it easier for me to spot which fancy bits weren't doing enough work.

And while I was revising my first two young adult novels, I played with rearranging my sentences to put the most important word last. (Partly because I knew people would be skimming a bit, and people always notice the final word in a sentence, but also for emphasis.) Like recently, I changed a sentence from:

"If she's caught inside the Compassion's headquarters, she'll be lost in ways she can't even imagine."

to:

"If she's caught inside the Compassion's headquarters, she can't even imagine all the ways she'll be lost."

This puts the emphasis on "lost," and feels more punchy and emotional to me—whereas ending on "imagine" feels more wistful.

I still fall into repetition and clunky constructions all the time, even in stuff that makes it all the way to publication—I'm working on getting better at catching this stuff, but my eye slides off it sometimes. At least I'm coming up with new and interesting ways to screw up.

You are sentenced to flow

The sentence is the basic unit of prose. When we talk about the flow of someone's writing, we're usually talking about the sentences. You can create a rhythm by alternating longer and shorter sentences, or using a bunch of long sentences to lead up to a very short sentence, or breaking up the sentence structure entirely. Sometimes, I'll try and mangle syntax on purpose, using a sentence fragment (a sentence without a proper verb, or even a noun) or a comma splice (two sentences smushed together, with a comma between them).

Each sentence should flow into the next, in terms of both meaning and music. You can tell how the end of one sentence sets up the beginning of the next, or how each sentence is kind of developing the same idea or telling you more about the same thing. Sentences shouldn't feel like they're bumping up against each other in a weird or unpleasant way—which can happen if, for example, multiple sentences begin with the same word or similar phrasing. Or if each sentence feels like a separate thought, and you can't see how they connect.

I think a lot about tempo, as well as dynamics, in the musical score I'm creating, meaning that I try to speed up and slow down the pace of the individual sentences. For an action sequence, I might have a bunch of really short choppy sentences that keep you skipping from action to action. For a scene-setting or mood-evoking sequence, I might use longer, rolling sentences, that hopefully lull you into a particular state of mind. Also, a more action-packed moment might require more emphasis on verbs and less on other parts of speech.

In the next chapter, we'll talk more about humor—but if you're trying to write funny prose, then a lot of your sentences are going to be set up for a sort of payoff. Not necessarily a "punch line," but some twist that comes after you've built up a picture in the reader's head. And meanwhile, if you're writing horror, a lot of your prose is going to be about engineering a sense of dread and anxiety, leading the reader inexorably toward some image that's going to fritz their biscuits.

Most of the time, you're trying to get the reader to notice, or remember, one thing in particular. Could be a piece of information, an action, an especially good joke, an emotional beat, or a revolting image. Whatever it is, all the little mechanics of each sentence, and the interplay of the sentences, need to set it up and deliver it.

One of the things I struggled with the most was breaking up the rhythm of my sentences, without messing everything up. If I decided I needed to add an extra moment or piece of information in the middle of an existing chunk of story, I couldn't see how to split that chunk into two pieces so I could insert something. I got hung up on the seamlessness of "this bit goes into this bit which goes into this bit." I needed lots of practice to be able to find the hidden seams inside a block of text that I could rip apart and then stitch back together with the new thing in between.

Finding your own style

There are a bunch of ways to figure out your own writing style, including ideas I've already mentioned, like using speech-to-text, writing longhand, and reading your work aloud to audiences. Listen to yourself talk, because the cadence of your speech can help guide the shape of your prose.

A lot depends on what kind of stories you're telling—not just genre, but content in general—and what sort of reaction you're trying to create in the reader's head. But also, keep fooling around! Try on different versions of your own style, with more ten-cent words, or fewer. See how dropping in short declarative paragraphs changes the feel of your writing. Play around with puns, cuss words, slang, words you made up, passive verbs and active verbs, and so on. Write only short Hemingway-esque sentences, or endless Faulknerian sentence-sprawls.

I learned a lot about fiction writing as a journalist, from editors who taught me to find the punchiest way to say something. Like instead of starting an article with "Deborah says the tourists have ruined her favorite spot," start with, "Deborah blames tourists for ruining . . ." But I also learned a lot from my econ professor, who forced me to write ultra-short executive summaries at the start of every paper.

But the thing that helped the most was ripping off other authors. It's a paradox: I found my personal writing style, that is unique to me alone, by stealing other writers' tricks. Read a variety of different authors, pay attention to the mechanics of their prose, and try copying them for a bit. Write a pastiche, even. Nobody will know, I promise.

A lot of writers seem superstitious about reading too much of a particular author, as if they'll end up just copying that person. And maybe that's happened to somebody. But I always feel like I've borrowed a little bit of someone else's mojo when I let their style sink in and influence me a bit, and I can always tone down the homage in revisions. Plus if you read a ton of Raymond Chandler one week and a ton of Samuel Delany the next, they'll both be in the mix somewhere.

I used to be a fast reader, but as I've struggled to get better at writing, my reading has slowed down, because I have to stop and really soak in a passage to see what's going on there, on a word-by-word basis. How is each sentence helping to create a particular effect, and what words does this author emphasize? And how?

Your style is the sum of countless little choices that you make, over and over. It's also the stuff you can't

SENTENCES ARE FULL OF POTHOLES

I try not to fall into a journalistic style when I'm doing personal essays or fiction. But my time in journalism did teach me something really vital: the importance of clarity above all.

I try to keep an eye out for potholes and confusing clutter in my sentences, though inevitably some of that stuff makes it to print. English is full of words that could be either verbs or nouns, for example, which increases the risk of a sentence being misread. The reader might think "land" is an action rather than an object, unless "land" is placed with care.

It's also easy, in English, to use a pronoun without being clear what it's referring to, like "He aimed his ray gun at the monster, but it was broken." (Was the monster broken, or the ray gun?) Sometimes I'll use the same preposition twice in two different ways, like "The room was filled with couches with gold leaf on their arms," and this can be confusing to parse.

Here's a sentence I wrote just recently: "I made all kinds of bargains with the universe in my head." I meant to say that I was making bargains with the universe within the privacy of my own thoughts, but you could easily read that sentence to mean that I had an entire cosmos crammed into my skull. On a similar tip, I try to keep words close to their modifiers. So instead of "He needed to get everything he had forsaken back," I'll write, "He needed to get back everything he had forsaken."

If there's any way to misread a sentence, you can be sure it will happen. The only solution I've found is to reread slowly and think about how to make it obvious which words are the subject, verb, and object in each sentence. And reading sentences out loud is always a valuable diagnostic, with or without an audience.

help doing, even if you make an effort to shift to a noir sensibility for a gritty pulp story, or a more verbose chatty narrator. Style is everything that becomes habit.

Once you have come up with your own style, you can easily get locked into it. Either through force of habit, or other people's expectations. So if you're still configuring your prose, enjoy the freedom to mess around.

CHAPTER 23

A Strong Narrator Can Help You Weave a Spell of Protection

Narration is the most magical part of creative writing—in fact, it's also the part that most closely resembles casting an actual spell. Say you're trapped in a dark wood, with a few drops of oil left in your lamp and slime-goblins closing in on all sides. You'll try to say the exact phrases, in the right order, that weave a whole reality around you, to ward off evil.

A strong narrator, with control over point of view, tone, and imagery, can wield an incredible mojo. As a reader, I usually fall in love with a story because I can tell that there's a Storyteller, who is not necessarily the same person as the author, guiding me forward from the very first line. I crave the sense that I'm in safe hands—like someone is scooping me up and carrying me along, perhaps placing me in their shirt pocket like a tiny mouse.

Every story has one or more narrators. This is true no matter whose point of view the story is being told from, or how it's being told. Different viewpoints make the narrator more or less apparent to the reader, and there's a spectrum, with "obnoxiously chatty" at one end and "barely there" at the end. A "tight" third person narrator, who sticks closely to the perceptions and thoughts of one character, may be almost invisible. But there's always someone, serving up events and images and dialogue in an artful fashion.

In previous chapters, we've talked about losing yourself in your plots, in your characters, in your worlds, and in big ideas and themes. But there is a special power in taking control over narration, because you can give yourself that same mouse-in-a-shirt-pocket feeling that makes reading such a unique pleasure. You can be swept along in your own telling of the story. Your narration style sets the expectation for what kind of tale you're writing. Is this thing going to be scary? Is it going to be funny? Am I going to cry a whole lot? All of the above? Every narrative includes a wealth of clues that help the reader sense what they're getting themself into. And yes, you can absolutely set an expectation that this'll be a cute comedy of manners and then unleash the nastiest hell on page 49, but that requires a certain amount of skill and delicacy (and foreshadowing) to avoid the feeling that you just lost control.

And really, it's all about control—both having control, and letting the reader know that you are in control, so the reader trusts that they won't fall out of this book and go splat.

Two of the main strings that let you puppeteer your narrator are point of view (POV), and tone.

It all depends who's telling the story, and how

POV is who's telling the story, and tone is how they're telling it. There are many different types of narrator, and they have different levels of intimacy and immediacy. The decisions you make about both POV and tone shape how close the reader gets to be to the events of the story.

A first-person narrator is telling you their own story as they experience(d) it, and I've found through trial and error that first-person narration feels much more immediate in present tense than in past tense. In present tense, a first-person narrator is telling you what's happening, as it happens: "I am being eaten by a sentient blob of nano glue, send help." Whereas in past tense, this "I" is telling you a story of something they already lived through—we know they (probably) came out okay, but they also have a certain amount of distance from the events they're describing. A lot of situations might seem intense and scary in the moment, but are funny when you think about them later.

Third-person past-tense narration might have less immediacy than first-person present tense—and yet *more* than first-person, past tense. This sounds counterintuitive—but think of the difference between "I couldn't breathe and my stomach was clenching," and "She couldn't breathe. Her stomach clenched." The third-person narrator is telling you the facts of what happened, without the gloss of "at the time, I was really scared." Meanwhile, a third-person, present tense narrator always feels a bit breathless and noir to me, maybe because that's where I've mostly encountered it.

I have to confess I haven't experimented much with second-person narration, but N.K. Jemisin uses it to great effect in *The Fifth Season*.

Tone, meanwhile, encompasses stuff like humor, drama, emotion, scariness, and other kinds of feelings that the prose might evoke. Your tone constrains the types of things that can happen in the story, and how they're described, and how we're going to feel about them.

Another way to think about tone is in terms of setting a mood: excitement, sadness, mourning, bracing for the worst, picking up the pieces, etc. A strong sense of tone will enable you to shift from one mood to another without it feeling jarring, and this can be a powerful tool—you can go from the thrills of the battle scene to the somber aftermath. Or jump from the giddy POV of someone who's in love and ready for her first dance with her beloved to the miserable viewpoint of someone who's just lost everything.

Your tone needs to be able to encompass a lot of different moods, and hold them all together as part of the same story. So you might be writing a funny story, or a whimsical one, but you can build in room for sadness and darkness by including hints of those things creeping in. And the transitions between moods need to be seamless, so the storytelling feels like it's all of a piece. Aang, in *Avatar: The Last Airbender,* can discover the burnt corpses of his fellow airbenders in one scene, and then be frolicking and joking around a few scenes later, because the show never loses that sense of childlike innocence and playfulness and fun, even when things get darker.

In television, one of the things that happens before an episode gets filmed is the "tone meeting," where the director gets together with a bunch of creative people to go through the script page by page. What is each scene about? What is the emotional content of the scene, and what stuff from previous episodes is lurking in the subtext? All of these things help to influence how the scene is shot and how lines are read. The tone, basically.

POV and tone shape each other

POV and tone are closely linked. Try to imagine if Arthur Dent was narrating the events of Douglas Adams' *The Hitchhiker's Guide to the Galaxy* in the first person—the humor would land very differently, and you wouldn't get all of those funny asides from the Guide. Either Arthur would need to have a lot more self-awareness and irony, or his endless complaining might get on your nerves after a while.

I recently read an old interview with Ray Bradbury, where he described himself as a type of movie director. He wrote as if he had a camera in his head, and he was showing you the story, shot by shot, and he encouraged Hollywood to use his stories almost as film scripts. And obviously, this approach works way better with an omniscient third-person narrator, who can see from any "camera angle."

On the other hand, *The Hunger Games* would lose a lot of its power if it was told in the third person. Just read that opening paragraph, and you're immediately steeped in Katniss' dread as the reaping day approaches. And this is true for a lot of other young adult novels that use first person and present tense to put you right in the skin of someone who's being swept up in the flow of events.

The personality of the narrator does a lot to shape your tone. A cheery, wisecracking narrator (either third person or first person) will make things lighter. A grim, tense narrator inevitably means a darker feel overall. Both POV and tone come out in the images the narrator uses, just like with the redbrick wall we talked about in chapter fifteen. A narrator who lingers on the cobwebs and grime all over a castle will create a different feeling than one who obsesses about all the lovely antique furniture strewn about the place. Your choice of metaphors, the style of the dialogue, and the descriptions of different actions all help to show the narrator's attitude. It's the difference between "rain spattered onto the filthy windowpane as she braced for another slash of lightning" and "the murmur of rainfall soothed me as I lay in bed."

At the same time, the events of the story will shape the tone—and vice versa. It's easy to think about the tone as just a decorative glaze that goes over the surface, without affecting the actual bones of the story. But see above: the tone sets your expectations, and each incident also clarifies the tone. A cute, whimsical romance can't necessarily incorporate a blood-spattering chainsaw rampage, any more than you'd expect a Busby Berkeley dance number in the middle of *Game of Thrones*.

I always struggle to incorporate humor, irony, and weirdness, without those things overwhelming the emotion and our investment in the characters. And tone is where that particular challenge comes together. With *All the Birds in the Sky*, for example, I wanted a whimsical tone that never spilled over into the sort of quirkiness that might require pizzicato violin music.

And the opening of *All the Birds in the Sky* was a huge challenge.

My original opening line was: "Once upon a time, there was a girl named Patricia."

Then I switched to: "Two little girls lived in an old spice mill in the woods."

Then: "When Patricia was six years old, she found a wounded bird in the forest, and it broke her heart."

That last one is pretty close to the final version. I kept hearing from my beta readers that the fairy-tale tone of the earlier openings made for a jarring lurch when the characters grew older and the story became more complex.

So I dialed back the "fairy-tale" feel of the opening, while trying to find subtle ways to telegraph that the story was going to get darker and more grown-up. And also, that even if we were starting out in Patricia's head, the third-person narrator would occasionally become somewhat omniscient. I hoped, as long as the tone remained whimsical-with-feels, people could hang on as I took some sharp turns.

Most stories have a cluster of tones, rather than one

You might find it helpful to think of tone as kind of a Venn diagram. Unless you're writing a really simple kind of story, you're going to have multiple moods or feelings, and your tone is the intersection between those things. Your scenes could be "scary," "romantic," "funny," and "sad," with more emphasis on each of those things, at different times.

The Venn diagram thing is useful, because the overlap between those different feelings is where your story really lives. The more you keep reverting to the middle, the intersection of those different feels, the stronger your sense of tone can be. If, most of the time, your tone is a little bit scary and a little bit funny, or a little bit romantic and a little bit sad, then you can more easily go all the way into full-on scariness or romance.

Since you can't be sure of what your tone needs to be until you have the events of the story set in stone, you'll probably have to adjust the tone in revision. In fact, I frequently will go back and change a story or novel from first person to third person, or vice versa, once I have a complete draft. (It's a pain in the butt, and there are always bits where I missed a stray "I" in a story that's morphed into third person.)

Don't worry if your tone wobbles or even strays wildly, in your first or even second draft. This is part of the fun! You're figuring out what's going to work, and what kind of story you're telling, and it could be a mistake to commit to one tone too quickly. Once you've got a finished draft, you'll probably be able to tell which moments go too far into satire or horror, and fall outside the tone that you've decided to set.

I'll often find that my earlier drafts go so wrong, in terms of tone, that it's pushed the story in a direction that I didn't really intend for it to go. A scene that should have

WRITING EXERCISE: SAME MOMENT, DIFFERENT TONES

Here's a fun experiment: come up with a brief scene (which could be in your current work-in-progress, or could be something you cook up from scratch). This could be anything: two characters meet for the first time, have an intense conversation, or say goodbye forever. Someone runs away from home, escapes from prison, or gets caught stealing a pen from a convenience store. Whatever catches your fancy.

Then try and write a paragraph of this vignette in four different tones and viewpoints. For example:

1. A funny, absurdist third-person POV, with a narrator who is pointing out odd facts, using intentionally ridiculous similes, or lampooning the foibles of your characters.

2. An introspective, reflective first-person narrator, who is trying to make sense of their complicated past, and to own all of their regrets and

triumphs. Lots of personal asides and reveries.

3. A grimdark, noir tone (which could be first or third person) that describes everything through a layer of grittiness. Including punchy dialogue, atmospheric description (grunge and rain and disreputable places!), and the most cynical word choices.

4. Laconic, matter-of-fact narration that leaves out unnecessary ornamentation, stripping everything down to just the major facts, but leaving room for a few startling images or descriptions of random items.

Those are just suggestions. You could also pick a recent book you've enjoyed, and try to copy its tone and POV. Or try to write the most intentionally purple prose you can, full of extra adjectives and adverbs. Write an experimental prose poem, or a soaring epic-fantasy voice, or a deliberately unreliable narrator who keeps changing their story.

Once you have four para-

been tender was spiky and angry, or a dramatic confrontation fell flat, and this meant that every scene that came afterward was heading in the wrong direction. All too often, when a story has gone off the rails, it's nothing to do with plot or character problems, per se—it's that I've swerved into a tone that doesn't serve the story I'm trying to tell.

Once I start getting a handle on my tone, usually in my second or third draft, I can use it to signpost not only what's happening, but what's going on beneath the surface. Little notes of description or scene-setting, or the transitions from one mood to another, can show the characters' subtext as well as all the thematic stuff that's lurking in the background. You can sometimes show a character's internal monologue without showing it—instead of having the character think, "I'm really pissed about what's happening," just show the scene through their eyes, and describe everything in a sarcastic or grouchy way.

Tone can include irony, satire, disruption, sadness, love, and all of the other modes of storytelling that let you tell a story that is defiantly real (or wonderfully surreal). When you find the right narrator, with the right personality, you'll find it easier to get swept up in your own story, when the "real" world is an endless river of sewage. Getting a handle on your narrator also makes it easier for you to be subversive, or sincere, or both—which, in turn, allows you to tell the stories that might help us all dig our way out of our collective mess. You can land an emotional gut punch by moving out of the center of that Venn diagram into one of the circles.

The greater control you have over your narrator, the more easily you can pull the rug out from under your reader, without losing their pocket-mouse trust in you.

graphs containing the same events in four different tones, look at how each version seems different. Do they still seem like the same events? Is the pacing the same, and do you find yourself emphasizing different things? This exercise is a fun way to see how your narration choices can change the story at a fundamental level.

Think of these different tones and styles as parts of your Swiss army knife. (Why are the Swiss so obsessed with armies and knives, when they're supposed to be neutral?) You have a stabby tool, but you also have a scrapey tool, a corkscrew, and a snippy tool. Each of them can help to solve problems in different ways.

CHAPTER 24

When the World Goes Loopy, You Can Become a Master of Time and Space

My favorite moment in *Starcrash*—the low-budget *Star Wars* knockoff—comes when Christopher Plummer shouts in an operatic voice, "Imperial battleship, halt the flow of time!" But long before the Emperor used this power against the evil Count Zarth Arn, every novelist already possessed this same capability.

Anyone who writes a story has total control over the passage of time. You get to show us the events you want us to see, in the order you want us to see them. You can spend a dozen pages on a single moment in someone's life, or let a hundred years pass in a paragraph. This mastery of the past and future is wondrous at the best of times, but it's especially therapeutic when everything is a giant obscene mess. At such times, the world feels as if it's moving too fast *and* too slow, and we're living in the future as well as the past. We have no way to control any of it—unless you have a blank document handy.

Many of my favorite authors, from David Mitchell to N.K. Jemisin, play with both structure and time. And for my money, remixing a story's timelines is one of the most satisfying aspects of writing. Structure can be a thing of beauty and a source of narrative pleasure, just as much as the snappiest dialogue or the most heartfelt character moment. There's no storytelling tool more powerful than controlling the overall shape of the narrative.

A lot of writing experts will tell you every work of fiction shares the same "three-act structure." I've always thought this is true, as far as it goes: every story has a beginning, a middle, and an end. And yet, pretty much all of my favorite books screw around with the order of events, or come shaped like puzzle boxes, or have seven separate "third acts." Like David Foster Wallace's *Infinite Jest* or Rebecca Roanhorse's *Black Sun,* which jump around in time, or Mary Doria Russell's *The Sparrow,* which intersperses two timelines that slowly converge.

Time is the one drug that absolutely everyone is hooked on. And fiction is the only place to get a really potent hit.

Why do you write like you're running in and out of time?

One of my favorite things about the musical *Hamilton* is how tricksy its pacing is. The Battle of Monmouth is dealt with in a few lines, and the song "Right Hand Man" covers a huge swathe of events. But in other songs, a single conversation is allowed to unspool in real time, and the party where Alexander Hamilton meets the Schuyler sisters is shown twice, from two different points of view.

This is nothing compared to the trickery that prose can accomplish.

A novel or short story can slow things down until we see every detail of a scene, with a clarity that might never exist elsewhere. Down to the dust motes swirling in a shaft of light from a half-open window, and the plate of glistening sticky buns that are right in the middle of toppling onto the floor. The written word also has the ability to summarize, carrying you through a long period of time without feeling like you're skipping over anything. ("Every day for six months, she taught him to read the bones and to taste the subtle variations in the flavor of human blood.")

A few years ago, I went to an event where Kim Stanley Robinson said this ability to elapse time, to create a feeling of living through something in just a few lines, is the greatest advantage of prose fiction over other media.

It's true: other media have their own ways of trying to high-light a particular moment, or to show visually that time is pass-ing, but when a narrator tells you about a long stretch of time, it's uniquely potent. Montages always feel clunky by compari-son, and so do slow dissolves. Likewise, no other medium can keep you in a single instant the way that prose can. A comic-book artist might draw a gorgeous two-page spread of a single image, but they can't prevent you from glancing and then turn-ing the page to see the next word balloon.

Your use of time, to a huge extent, shapes the meaning of your story. Things that you choose to linger over automatically take on more meaning and emotional significance, especially if we're see-ing them through the eyes of someone who cares about them (or hates them). You can make us believe that two people have deep-ened their relationship over a long period of time, without forcing us to witness every conversation about where to have lunch.

To some extent, being aware of the passage of time in your story is a matter of not boring the reader by plodding forward. Yet keeping a finger on the pitch control of the universe is also a way to infuse everything with greater meaning and excitement—and also a good start on one of the toughest aspects of writing: pace.

Pace yourself

Every novel I've ever written has dragged in the middle, at least according to my beta readers. I always get to a certain point in the story and want to poke around and explore my fictional world, and have lots of meandering conversations about noth-ing in particular.

I never solved these problems by cutting out all the conversa-tions, or the exploration. Instead, I combined two or three scenes into one, or tightened them up, or found ways to make a static scene feel more dynamic. Instead of showing someone getting out of their car, walking inside a building, and getting in the elevator, I jump straight to them walking inside their apartment.

A lot of pacing is creating the sense that something is happening, even if that "something" is just "we're caught in the rain without an umbrella." A sequence where someone buys a hat can feel fast-moving and exciting, if we care about the hat in question, and if each moment of the hat-buying has something interesting going on. And if nothing feels repetitive or redundant. Conversely, you could write a giant battle scene, involving countless decapitations, betrayals, and reversals, that feels as though nothing is really happening. "Oh, another decapitation. Yawn—wake me when someone buys a hat."

As long as suspense is building, and the reader can tell that the walls are slowly closing in on the characters, we can put up with a lot of slow scenes. Watching two people argue about whether Kant's universal law truly applies to the entire universe (including places where cause-and-effect operate quite differently) can be downright thrilling, if you know there's a monster sneaking up on them. Or if they're having this debate while breaking into an evil fortress.

Most people I know read for feels, as much as for clever plot twists or awesome fight scenes. And these things all make each other more interesting and punchy, so to speak.

Also, the more balls you can keep in the air, the faster the pace will feel, because the reader will be aware of all the other balls over your head while you're catching one of them.

Another reason your pacing might feel wonky, incidentally: things might not be happening too quickly or too slowly, but just at the wrong time or in the wrong order. All too often, I've realized that the problem with a story was that the characters learned a key piece of information too early, sapping the story of its urgency or moving it toward the climax too soon. Or a key event happened in the middle of a dozen other things, rather than when it would have the most impact.

This is one reason why I always outline a story or novel after I've written one or two complete drafts. I think about the turning points in the story, and try to space them out so that each turning point has enough time to sink in, before the status quo gets reversed again.

I'll even assign a word-count target to each section of a book, to ensure that nothing is overstaying its welcome. Assuming a novel is going to be roughly 100,000 words total and there are five sections, I try to keep each section around 20,000. (Or I might decide that two of the five sections can be 15,000 words, allowing two others to be 25,000 each.) If one section is going way over its goal, I may have to cut or tighten some of my favorite scenes.

This technique probably won't work for everyone, but I find it imposes a certain amount of discipline and forces me to think about what percentage of a book's running length I want to spend on a particular place or series of events. If something is one-fifth of the story, maybe it should only be one-fifth of the book. (Though of course, you could also decide that the section that's currently occupying 40 percent of your word count is a bigger piece of the story than you'd realized—I'm not saying you need to be rigid about this stuff, at all.)

This is just one of the ways that structure can help you clarify what matters in your story.

Structure can be tremendously healing

Your structure is also a chance to build something meaningful into the foundations of your work, shaping the experience of the readers and characters. A cool structure can help you highlight things in your story, create more suspense, or just make sure that you build to a banging conclusion where everything comes together just right. For example, in *The Sparrow,* the two alternating timelines add more significance to each other.

Sometimes I'll write a story in chronological order, and then decide it should really start in the middle instead, because that's the most interesting jumping-off point. Then I'll take everything leading up to that midpoint, and turn it into a series of flashbacks, intercut with the story's present.

Different types of structure mean different things. In the above example, telling the story linearly would give us the whole journey of how the characters got to where they are. That way, we see the experiences and choices that drew them into a situation, and then we see that situation unfold with the full knowledge of how we got there. Interspersing the present with a series of flashbacks, meanwhile, lets you juxtapose events from the two time periods.

Juxtaposition is the heart of irony, and playfulness, and meta narration. Placing someone's infancy directly alongside their old age lets you draw connections, create resonances, or show more clearly the things that have shaped this person's life. You can use this contrapuntal structure, and the ability to rewind and fast-forward, to show the things that your characters are willfully overlooking, or to increase the weirdness and surrealism in your story. Like with the party where Hamilton meets Eliza and Angelica, you can show the same event from multiple angles, or different perspectives. You can have a tight focus on one tiny thing—and then pull way back, and show the bigger picture.

The frame around your story is often the most political part, too, because it's about excluding some things and highlighting others. Oppressive ideologies often depend on keeping a para-noiacally narrow frame, so you don't see who's been left out of the picture, or you don't grasp the larger historical context behind a grindingly awful system.

Structure is also beautiful in its own right. A conscious approach to structure can be tremendously soothing, like crafting a puzzle box, or building a scale model of Versailles. One of my favorite things to do, in a short story or a novel, is to put something game-changing at the exact midpoint, and then make the first half and the second half mirror each other. If the ending feels like a reflection of the beginning, then this symmetry can add to the sense that you've gone somewhere, and come back again.

I'm also a big fan of time jumps, where a dozen years pass between sentences, and of false climaxes, where events reach a narrative peak only to subside again. And you gotta love a structure in which there's one central event, which we don't get to see until the very end of the story, but we can tell that we're getting closer and closer to it, even as we jump around in time.

To return to pacing, most stories need to have a sense of "rising action." For the climax to have any impact, it has to feel like the tension has been ratcheted up and up, until the story finally gets to the point where everything is at a crisis. I usually feel like every story has a point where it stops pushing uphill, and starts rolling downhill. Events are spiraling out of control, or everything that's happened up till now has built up an unstoppable momentum. The characters will do whatever it takes to get answers, or to solve their problems, and everything speeds up.

So a good structure will not only let the reader know what the big turning points in the story are, but show how the consequences of those turning points are piling up. This is a big part of why I say the ending is the beginning: once you have an ending that you love, that feels like it pays off the themes and the character arcs of your whole story, then you can go back and shape all that raw material into something where every moment serves to build up power that you can discharge at the end.

CHAPTER 25

Irony Doesn't Have to Be the Enemy of Feels. They Can Team Up, in Fact!

When I think about the stories that have gotten me through the worst times in the world, two seemingly opposite powers come to mind:

- They've given me the tools to rise up and see the walls of the maze from a great height.
- They've helped me to get deeper into someone else's skin and see their perspective, and maybe helped me to believe in the power of human connection.

In other words, irony and empathy.

People talk about irony as if it's some sort of arch, eyebrow-raising postmodern exercise in saying that nothing means anything. Or even matters. Irony has also been tarnished, in recent years, by the swarm of bottom-feeders being "ironically racist" and/or "ironically misogynistic."

Used skillfully, irony can become a tool of subversion against the powerful, revealing truths that are messy or hidden. As anyone who's ever seen a clever quote-tweet knows, irony can expose hypocrisy and point out the flaws in the logic of our meritocratically chosen elites. (My use of the term "meritocratically chosen" is ironic, of course.)

Like I said last time, juxtaposition is the heart of irony. Just compare the high-minded speeches of politicians with the reality of their actions, or reveal the direct contrast between someone's actions in two different situations. Irony is about shifts in perspective, redrawing the lines. I live for that shit, especially in fiction. This is one reason why I push back so hard against writing experts who insist there's only one right way to handle POV, or that you can't show more than one person's point of view in a single chapter.

Empathy, meanwhile, includes a couple of vital tasks: 1) Showing the humanity (or personhood) of a bunch of characters, including people who might not seem sympathetic at first. Nobody is an NPC, everybody has thoughts and dreams and random food cravings. 2) Modeling empathy among your characters and showing how people can understand each other in spite of all the totally valid reasons to get stabby.

There's a reason this book started by talking about big themes and ended up talking about nuts-and-bolts stuff like perspective, narration, pacing, and structure. You can't achieve the liberation that those early essays promise without the full toolkit: the ability to control the focus of the story so that you can show contrasts, highlight certain moments, and shift perspectives at will.

Empathy and irony might appear at first to be opposites, or mutually exclusive. One is about getting right inside someone's state of mind and revealing the contents of their heart. The other is about pulling back, until you expose the disconnects between reality and what someone believes.

But the empathic and the ironic modes can easily coexist—in fact, they work great together. The more keenly we feel someone's yearning or rage, the sharper the effect when we see what they're missing or willfully ignoring. I often think about the famous scene in Henry Fielding's *The History of Tom Jones, a Foundling* when Mrs. Waters is determined to seduce Tom over dinner, but the ravenously hungry Tom is obsessed with his food—Fielding gives us both perspectives at once through a mock-heroic narration, so we sympathize with these two (temporarily) incompatible hungers at the same time.

How to get deep

The first step in being able to empathize with your characters is to get out of the way. You can't generate empathy if you're constantly judging your characters, revealing their utter hypocrisy, and undercutting all their motivations. Let them feel what they feel, without constantly imposing your own opinions.

This is where POV and narration come in: the stronger your control over these things, the deeper you can crawl inside someone's mental state. With a first-person narrator, everything hangs on how well you capture their voice and infuse every word with the intensity of their anxieties and dreams. With a third-person narrator, it's all about capturing someone's internal monologue with as little filter as possible.

I've also learned the hard way not to let my sense of humor, or my love of weirdness, undercut the characters.

I had one short story, a few years ago, which I couldn't finish, even though I really liked the first two-thirds and felt like it had no shortage of potential. I kept poking at it for months, trying to figure out what I needed to add to make it work—until I realized all I had to do was cut one scene, which revealed that my main character was a terrible person despite being written in her POV. That scene was making it impossible for me to invest fully in that character, and also wrecking my belief in her perspective, even though it cracked me up. As soon as that scene was gone, I was all in for this character, and I saw exactly how to end their story.

In earlier drafts of *All the Birds in the Sky,* there were many places where I kept throwing the characters under the bus for the sake of a joke. I had to go through, systematically, and make sure that the humor wasn't coming at the expense of Laurence or Patricia. I had a funny line in a scene where Laurence is talking to his girlfriend Serafina:

"Laurence tried to fill the silence with more active listening."

This felt as if the narrator was making fun of Laurence, so I eventually switched it so Laurence himself was thinking:

"I wish I could use active listening to fill the silence."

Not a big change—but it kept us in Laurence's perspective.

Writing a young adult novel, in first person, was really good for me. I gathered up my favorite YA books and spread them out around me on the floor. I sat for hours, paging through them and trying to see how they beamed emotion and urgency directly into my brain. I wanted the narrative voice of *Victories Greater Than Death* to be wisecracking and funny, but also passionate, idealistic, outraged, terrified. I obsessively studied the narration in books by Holly Black, Suzanne Collins, Bethany C. Morrow, and Tracy Deonn, among others.

Took me a dozen drafts before I got Tina saying things like, "I feel frozen to the marrow, like I've waded neck-deep into a lake on the bleakest day of winter," but also "I buy spicy chips and ultra-caffeinated sodas, the perfect fuel for confronting ass-hattery (ass-millinery?)."

A lot of it comes down to laughing (or screaming) with your characters, rather than at them.

Like I said before, I read for human connection. Seeing people have empathy for each other is one of the best ways to develop empathy for them. There's a reason why "enemies to friends" is such a huge trope—we all want to believe that people can learn to understand each other, and that a strong negative emotion can soften into something more nurturing. Plus of course, sweetness is always sweeter when it replaces bitterness.

Irony can be incredibly lazy

We live in a moment where pop culture is drenched in a bland, reflexive irony. Even before we had exhaustive online catalogues of tropes, we were all dreadfully familiar with the former assassin/spy who gets interrupted in their secluded cabin, to be summoned on One Last Mission. We all knew by heart the story of an older college professor who has an affair with one of his grad students. *The Simpsons* taught us to lampoon the cop who dies tragically the day before they're supposed to retire.

We're marinating in this hyper-awareness of clichés, and meanwhile we're constantly hearing that every story has already been told. (Which is true as far as it goes—there are an infinite number of untold stories, but they will inevitably share some basic characteristics with the ones that already exist.) So it's tempting to fall into a "sophisticated" state of dissociation, where all stories are inherently derivative and pointless. Tempting, but lazy.

At its worst, this leads to self-aware narrative karaoke: off-key cover versions of someone else's greatest hits, delivered with a giant wink that says we're all too cool to care about any of this noise. (More on that in the next chapter!)

The answer isn't to avoid irony, but to replace stale irony with a fresher variety. Make every situation feel brand-new, by pouring emotion and vivid details and a strong point of view into each word, and then draw back the curtain and show the rest of the picture that undermines, or complicates, what we just saw.

Irony works better if we care

Irony doesn't have to be particularly funny, as Kurt Vonnegut proved. For years, I'd been thinking of Vonnegut as a comic writer, but then I went back and reread a big chunk of *Breakfast of Champions* and discovered an angry, sarcastic misanthrope who uses devices like defamiliarization (i.e., explaining things we already know about as if we'd never heard of them) to jar us out of our complacency and certainty.

My favorite type of irony is poignant, sad, and weird, because the folly that's being exposed is tragic. I also love it when a story encourages us to laugh at a pathetic character, until we unexpectedly sympathize with their downfall—like poor Malvolio in Shakespeare's *Twelfth Night,* with his yellow garters.

Another way to make irony better: subvert the characters' expectations, rather than the audience's. It's very easy to fool an audience, who only know what you tell them. Like the countless movies and TV shows where you think the cops are about to burst into a basement where someone is held captive, because of clever editing and framing, but then the squad rushes into an empty cellar, and meanwhile the captive is still alone. It's way more satisfying, though harder to pull off, if a character believes something and then has the rug pulled out from under them.

I also think hard about which characters in the story are allowed to have real interior lives, and which ones are having what I call "comedy feelings" (i.e., feelings that are heightened and exaggerated and usually very id-based). Like, I've just been watching the *Harley Quinn* animated show, and it's noticeable that only Harley and Poison Ivy are allowed to have complex interiority. Everyone else has feelings that are played exclusively for laughs.

I've found over and over that I get a lot of mileage from stopping and drilling down into the head of a hitherto one-dimensional supporting character. When I flip things around and try to see the whole story from the POV of the sidekick, or the henchperson, or the antagonist, I can peel off a whole extra layer of significance. That's a type of irony that can be both poignant and kinda jarring.

(And the question of whom we're allowed to identify with in fiction is a highly political one—when women, BIPOC people, and other marginalized groups are always ciphers, or always relegated to having "comedy feelings," this becomes a self-reinforcing spiral of othering.)

Playing with tone and perspective and time and voice is a way to make the story more interesting, and maybe to push it into a more efficient shape. But those same tricks can also help you to balance ironic distance with emotional insights.

When you create a story, you're aiming to elicit a response from the reader. You want someone to laugh, freak out, scream, get verklempt. Generally, you get those reactions either by focusing on your characters and their feelings, making them as intense on the page as you can, or by making the reader aware that you, the author, are dancing a fancy dance. Those are both excellent ways to create a reaction—and the great news is, you don't have to choose between them. You can give us emotive protagonists and authorial soft-shoe, in the same story.

Just as long as your dancing doesn't step too heavily on your characters' toes.

CHAPTER 26

Write the Book That Only You Could Have Written

Several years ago, I was facing a tough choice. I had finished a hardboiled urban fantasy novel, which paid homage to Chandler, Hammett, Macdonald, and even Spillane, but also recent stuff like Richard Kadrey's Sandman Slim books. Everyone said I had a decent shot at getting a book deal for that novel, which was tentatively called *The Witch-Killers*. But meanwhile I had this *other* novel that I was halfway through writing, about a witch and a mad scientist who become friends, and maybe more.

There was a lot to like about both of those books. And yet, the more I thought about it the more I felt like *All the Birds in the Sky* was a better book to put out into the world. There were a bunch of reasons for this, but it boiled down to my sense that *All the Birds in the Sky* was a book that only I could have written. And you could kind of tell that *The Witch-Killers* was my attempt to copy Kadrey, Jim Butcher, Seanan McGuire, or countless others. Not to mention, I was chasing a trend that was already coming to a close.

When I look back at *The Witch-Killers,* it's clear I made the right choice. That novel feels more derivative than ever, and it's already severely dated. I'm also embarrassed by how much I let my love of noir push me into some unfortunate tropes. The main female character is half femme fatale, half damsel in distress, and the protagonist feels a bit like a stock tough-guy character. *All the Birds* was clearly a stronger choice for a major-label debut.

To be clear, I still steal liberally from my icons. Anyone who reads my stuff will see Chandler in there, mixed with Doris

Lessing, Ursula K. Le Guin, Octavia Butler, Iain M. Banks, and many others. I wear my influences all over both of my sleeves, but I also try to make them my own. As with everything else about writing, this is totally subjective, and boils down to nebulous stuff like personality. My "personality" as a writer is not particularly noir, even if I dip into that mode from time to time.

So my final piece of advice is: write the book that only you could have written.

Don't write what you hope will be popular, or what other people think is cool. Don't try and follow some formula that someone else said is the perfect storytelling Mad Libs, where X always happens on page 31. Don't chase trends. Or try to jump on someone else's success, unless you're like, "Wow, I always wished I could write that, and now there's a market for it."

The times I've been happiest writing have been the ones when I was doing something that felt super personal, like I was putting a piece of myself out into the world. (Even if it was a book about space pirates and goblins. Especially then.) My favorite projects are the ones that keep me thinking, "I don't know if I can pull this off—I don't know if anyone could—but I'm having a blast trying." I've always been aware some people would hate these misfit toys no matter how well they turned out, but I also couldn't help believing some people, the right people, would *really* love them.

I adore when my brain, my heart, and my gut flora conspire to do something that's uniquely my jam. And that doesn't mean it has to be literary or experimental or fancy—in fact, this is even more important if I'm writing a romance about the nine kings of asteroidland.

To this day, I'll often find myself reading a book and think to myself, "God, I wish I could write like this." I'll find some perfect turn of phrase, or a gorgeous scene, and feel a mix of admiration and envy. At such times, I do two seemingly contradictory things: I study what that other writer is doing, to learn what I can from it. And I remind myself that there are as many different types of good writing as there are writers, and it would suck if everybody wrote the same.

If someone else is experiencing success or acclaim writing stories where the only punctuation is semicolons, it's easy to feel as if you need to copy them. That's silly; semicolons are *their* thing; find your own thing.

Writing better means getting to know yourself

These essays have been about the power of creative writing to help you deal with turmoil and anxiety—but making up stories doesn't just help you to save yourself, but also to discover yourself.

When I look back at the fiction I wrote years ago, I see the person I used to be. When I think about the stories and novels I want to write next, I imagine the person I hope to become. I can't separate my personal evolution from my development as a writer, and I wouldn't want to be able to.

If I dig enough layers down, I can find the fiction I wrote when I still tried to live as a man. But also: stories that remind me of relationships that broke up long enough ago that those exes are hardly even exes anymore, just old friends. Fiction about the years I spent singing in church choirs, whole story cycles from when I was trying to be a buttoned-down financial journalist.

We talk as if getting better at writing were a continuous process of improvement—like today, you'll make a widget that's slightly better than the widget you made yesterday, until you asymptotically approach the platonic ideal of widgetness. But my experience is that I have good days and bad days, and ups and downs, and every time I feel like I've "leveled up" as a writer, I get worse again (often, the moment I start on a new project).

The longer I go on, the more it feels as if I haven't actually gotten better at writing—I've just gotten a bit more experience at spotting my own bullshit. I know that I have a tendency to go for the cheap joke instead of realness, for example, and I sometimes take lazy shortcuts. I also know my own strengths better, and I've seen those strengths change over time as I've developed as a person aside from my writing. Getting more aware of my own failings and capabilities has, in effect, made me stronger and more self-aware.

There's more to it than that, though. The longer I write and make countless tiny decisions, from "What happens next?" to "Who cleans the toilets in this world?", the more I understand how my own mind functions. Like a musical instrument that I've been tuning for years, and learning all its little quirks. Everything, from your characters to your themes to your narrative voice, is a reflection of who you are and how you think.

The other thing that happens after you've been writing for a while is that you have to be more careful not to repeat yourself too much (or to repeat yourself in interesting ways), which also requires paying attention, and knowing how to play the same notes differently on that same old instrument.

Earlier, I said that when you're figuring out what story you want to write, you should think about the stories you enjoy reading, or wish you could read. But eventually, you can also think about all those choices you've made in the past, and how they add up to a personality, which gives you a lens through which you can view all those potential stories. (Though, just like in real life, your writerly personality can encompass multiple modes and moods: nobody is ever jovial or grouchy all the time. When I talk about your personality, I'm not saying you need to write the same thing, the same way, all the time. You can be all three-dimensional and shit.)

To paraphrase Jean-Luc Picard in *Star Trek: The Next*

Generation "The Neutral Zone," the challenge is to improve yourself and enrich yourself, but also to discover yourself. Enjoy it.

Write the Book that Feels Close to Your Heart

For sure, part of the joy of writing is trying out different things. I'm always looking to stretch myself and find new challenges, and I actively try to develop the areas where I'm weakest as a writer. But meanwhile, I have also gotten more Marie Kondo about my writing projects: if something doesn't spark joy, why am I spending so much tears and brainjuice on it? More and more, I try to work on things that seem to have a direct line to the bottom of my psyche.

As I said before, the themes in your work are usually a reflection of your life or your own obsessions. And just like Jared Padalecki, you have to reach for the emotional truth of your own experiences to capture and convey something that feels real. You're always going to be putting something of yourself into your writing, even if you just set out to copy someone else wholesale. My happiest times as a writer have always been when I look at what I'm putting down and think, "this speaks *to* me, and *for* me."

People throw around old saws like "Write what you know," which are easily misinterpreted to mean "You can only write thinly veiled autobiography." But oftentimes, those phrases are really saying that you have to draw on your own experiences in your writing, even if you end up twisting them into something totally different. That shitty restaurant job you had during college can easily transform into the story of a hench-person working for a mediocre supervillain, for example, because those two situations are not dissimilar.

A lot of the most captivating writing is about hunger: for

a world, or a character, or a feeling. All of the chapters before this one have, in various ways, been about trying to connect with that hunger, and to feed it, so you can feel nourished even when the outside world is trying to starve you. So in this final chapter, I want to leave you with the idea that creative writing isn't just a way to survive—it's a way to become more yourself, and to share more of yourself with the world.

Good writing is in the eye of the beholder, and you'll never write something that leaves absolutely every reader saying, "This slaps." But you can write stories and personal essays and novels and model-rocket instructions that feel uniquely yours, and that make you feel a little closer to creative self-actualization. One of the great benefits of being a creative writer is that nobody will ever tell you that you're too self-absorbed (at least, while you're writing. At the grocery store, you're on your own).

Last and most importantly, do not forget to have fun. Word wrangling can be a slog and a pain and a huge source of anxiety and insecurity, but it can also be incredibly fun. Like, smashing-action-figures-together fun. Or cafeteria-food-fight fun. You get to write whatever you want, and stage ginormous disasters and explosions and chase scenes and dance numbers, and nobody can tell you to stop. Treasure those moments when you're on a tear, creating something unique and unbelievable, and completely your brainchild.

You got this. You're going to make something that nobody else could ever have come up with. When the bad times are over, you're going to emerge with your selfhood not just intact, but emblazoned like a heraldic crest across the fabric of your brand-new creation. I cannot wait to bear witness.

ACKNOWLEDGMENTS

I still can't believe that I got away with this reckless scheme—putting together a whole book of writing-advice essays and publishing them in real time at *Tor.com,* in the midst of a whole nut-cluster of apocalyptic scenarios.

When I brought this idea to Russ Galen, my agent did not flinch at the overweening (and underweening, and let's be honest sideways-weening) hubris of my design—instead, he rolled up his sleeves and figured out how to make it a reality. Patrick Nielsen Hayden was incredibly generous, both in facilitating this venture and in thoughtfully editing every one of these essays on a tight schedule.

There are so many other people at Tordotcom Publishing who were indispensable—and I apologize if I forget some names. Bridget McGovern, Irene Gallo, Chris Lough, Kenya Walker, Sanaa Ali-Virani, Molly McGhee, Miriam Weinberg, Oliver Dougherty, and countless others worked ridiculously hard to publish this book and deal with comments. Thanks so much also to Amanda Hong, who copyedited this book and made my prose shine way brighter.

Nisi Shawl, Claire Light, Na'amen Gobert Tilahun, Justina Ireland, and a few others gave me essential feedback on Chapter 21 of this book—and Nisi wrote a wonderful essay in response, which you can read at *Tor.com* (www.tor.com/2020/10/27/how -not-to-be-all-about-what-its-not-all-about-further-thoughts -on-writing-about-someone-elses-culture-and-experience). I'm also intensely grateful to everyone who commented on these essays at *Tor.com* or via social media, and especially to Alyx Dellamonica for all her encouragement.

This series started as a talk (also called "Never Say You Can't Survive"), which I gave at the Willamette Writers Conference, the Tucson Festival of Books, the Virginia G. Piper Center for Creative Writing, Boston University, and the Toronto Public Library. Thanks to Kate Thomas and everyone else who gave me feedback after hearing this talk.

When I was first writing that talk, I had lunch with Daphne Gottlieb, and she did a lot to help me figure out the big ideas—many of the smartest bits in this book came directly from that conversation with Daphne, who's a storytelling genius.

Annalee Newitz, my partner, encouraged me to do writing-advice essays at *io9,* back when we both worked on that site. And their insights and flights of fancy and ideas have shaped my ideas about writing and given me the heart to keep going. As much as creative writing may have helped me to survive rough times, I have no idea where I would be right now without Annalee's beautiful heart and mind.